DOWNHILL ALL THE WAY

Walking with Donkeys on the Stevenson Trail

DOWNHILL ALL THE WAY

Walking with Donkeys on the Stevenson Trail

HILARY MACASKILL AND MOLLY WOOD

DRAWINGS BY MOLLY WOOD

Best Wishes

from

Molly Wood

Hilary Macaskill

FRANCES LINCOLN

DOWNHILL ALL THE WAY
Frances Lincoln Limited
4 Torriano Mews
Torriano Avenue
London NW5 2RZ
www.franceslincoln.com

First Frances Lincoln edition: 2006

ISBN 10: 0-7112-2592-3
ISBN 13: 978-0-7112-2592-3

Printed and bound in Singapore
by KHL Printing Co Pte Ltd

2 4 6 8 9 7 5 3 1

*Frontispiece: Kenneth by the Mirandol viaduct, which
was being built when Stevenson was there.*

CONTENTS

CAST OF CHARACTERS

Gilles   Dynamic donkey-hirer from Pradelles on the Stevenson Trail. He is married to Suzanne and runs the Brasserie du Musée as well as a riding school and the *gîte d'étape*.

Suzanne   Married to Gilles, she helps run the Brasserie du Musée and the *gîte* at Pradelles. She walked part (the wet part) of taking the donkeys down to winter pasture.

Robert   Gilles' brother. Retired. Came to help walk the donkeys down to winter pasture. His wife doesn't like donkeys so we never saw her.

Bruno   Gilles' son who came to pick up Hilary and Molly from St Étienne Vallée Française and then fell asleep at the wheel so Molly had to drive, thereby discovering the van had no real brakes, which was quite frightening but it was the last time we went in it so no harm done.

Henri   Neighbour of Jacques and Odette who walked part (a very small part) of taking the donkeys down to winter pasture.

Jacques   Married to Odette, Suzanne's best friend. Jacques is a farmer and has a wonky hip.

Odette   Suzanne's best friend and married to Jacques. Came to help walk the donkeys down to winter pasture.

Valérie   Helper in the brasserie and at the riding school. She also helped walk the donkeys down to winter pasture.

Véro	Friend of Molly. Artistic person who used to work in a chemist's shop but now paints and decorates furniture.
Dany	Friend of Molly from tai chi class. Worked in a high-class jewellers in Montpellier.
Clive	Long-standing friend of Molly who introduced her to the Stevenson Trail. Before retirement, Clive was a diplomat and so got to know a lot about wine.
Auriol	Married to Clive. Does not like walking so her contribution to the Stevenson Trail was to drive the car to pick Clive up and chauffeur him to gastronomic delights elsewhere.
Florence	Friend of Molly from work. Florence has a horse and so knows about horses and donkeys and such.
Michèle	Friend of Molly from swimming class. Very fit person who is used to long-distance walking at high speed.
Michel	Friend of Dany and hotel owner at La Bastide Puylaurent. After flirting with the idea of making his hotel a donkey stop he has now plumped for quad bikes instead, so if you're a quad bike fan, his hotel is for you.

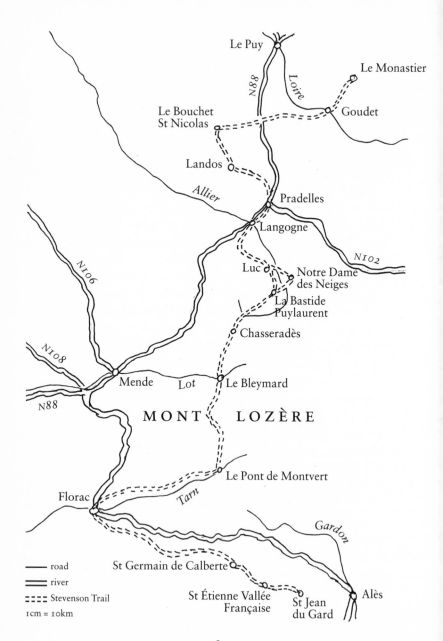

Le Puy

Le Monastier

N88

Loire

Le Bouchet
St Nicolas

Goudet

Landos

Allier

Pradelles

Langogne

N102

Luc

Notre Dame
des Neiges

La Bastide
Puylaurent

N106

Chasseradès

N108

Mende

Lot

Le Bleymard

N88

MONT   LOZÈRE

Le Pont de Montvert

Florac

Tarn

Gardon

road
river
Stevenson Trail
1cm = 10km

St Germain de Calberte

Alès

St Étienne Vallée
Française

St Jean
du Gard

WHY WERE WE HERE?

*In which Hilary looks back on treasured moments spent with
Molly the friend, Kenneth the donkey and Whiskey the dog*

'Water drummed down, bouncing off the forest floor. The
track ahead was obscured by mist. Thunder cracked and
rolled directly overhead; lightning forked vividly and demonically across the sky. We toiled up through woods that seemed
to be the site of a recent cyclone – branches and tree trunks
were strewn wildly across the path. Kenneth's hooves slipped
and slid as we negotiated our way round the obstacles.
Kenneth wasn't happy. Neither were we. We stopped to eat
the remains of the fruitcake. Molly rested her head exhaustedly on Kenneth's flank. We didn't exchange quips. We didn't
talk at all.

'When we got to the top of Col de la Planette, on the level
at last, it should have been easier going. But it wasn't.
Exposed as we were, it was much more difficult. It began to
hail, large hard lumps striking diagonally, lancing into us.
The wind was in full spate, buffeting us as we struggled to
keep our balance and the donkey under control. Over and
over again, Kenneth turned sideways, trying to get his back
into the storm and wind. Even Whiskey – ever cheerful – lost
his bounce, trotting miserably behind, tail dipped. Up there,
even the beech trees were cowed, clinging low to the ground
in an effort to escape the blast and, in this harsh environment,
barely in bud.'

Robert Louis Stevenson had the same sort of trouble. . . .

Left: The Stevenson Trail from top to bottom.

WHY WAS HE HERE?

In which Robert Louis Stevenson looks back
on similar times with Modestine the donkey

Alas, and I was on the brink of new and greater miseries! Suddenly, at a single swoop, the night fell. I have been abroad in many a black night, but never in a blacker. A glimmer of rocks, a glimmer of the track where it was well beaten, a certain fleecy density, or night within night, for a tree, – this was all that I could discriminate. The sky was simply darkness overhead; even the flying clouds pursued their way invisibly to human eyesight. I could not distinguish my hand at arm's length from the track, nor my goad, at the same distance, from the meadows or the sky.

Soon the road that I was following split, after the fashion of the country, into three or four in a piece of rocky meadow. Since Modestine had shown such a fancy for beaten roads, I tried her instinct in this predicament. But the instinct of an ass is what might be expected from the name; in half a minute she was clambering round and round among some boulders, as lost a donkey as you would wish to see. I should have camped long before had I been properly provided; but as this was to be so short a stage, I had brought no wine, no bread for myself and little over a pound for my lady-friend. Add to this, that I and Modestine were both handsomely wetted by the showers. But now, if I could have found some water, I should have camped at once in spite of all. Water, however, being entirely absent, except in the form of rain, I determined to return to Fouzilhic.

Robert Louis Stevenson,
Travels with a Donkey in the Cévennes, 1878

IF IT WAS THAT BAD, WHY DID HE DO IT? AND, COME TO THAT, WHY DID WE DO IT?

In which Molly explains

It all started for us when I went to see Hilary, who was spending a week in a friend's holiday home in the wilds of rural France, not too far from where I live. After lunch we went for a walk and I happened to mention that for the last few years I'd been searching for someone to walk the Stevenson Trail with me. A friend had talked about it and it appealed to my imagination but no one I knew at the time was interested in walking any further than to and from the car. As it happened, Hilary had picked up a very attractive leaflet the day before about hiring donkeys. We sat in the sunshine on the banks of a little stream, watching my dog playing in the water, and decided it would be a good thing to do. Then we took a shortcut back to the house to tell Hilary's husband and daughter, and got lost in thick undergrowth at the side of the stream. We finally emerged in the middle of a nursery on the other side of the village and had to pick our way daintily through rows of infant plants while the dog chased blue butterflies. Once out of the nursery (fortunately it was Sunday so no one saw us clambering about in the seedlings) we toiled back up the hill to a nice cup of tea and a piece of home-made cake. All the ingredients of the Stevenson Trail were already there: misplaced optimism in our map-reading/path-finding/orientation skills, fleeting but magical moments of natural beauty, greater physical exertion than we'd bargained for, and greedy guzzling of good things at the end of the day.

Things were more difficult for Robert Louis Stevenson. He founded the Stevenson Trail in 1878 simply by going for a walk and, hey presto, behind him stretched the Stevenson Trail. It was not recognised as such until more than a hundred years later when the French tourist authority caught up with him, but RLS had done his bit. He had wandered around in the Cévennes, a remote mountain range in the Massif Central region, for twelve days or so, armed with a donkey, a large two-person sleeping bag (ever-hopeful) and such useful items as a bottle of brandy, a leg of lamb and some dry bread. His immediate aim in doing so was to calm his mind while waiting to find out if the love of his life (an American woman called Fanny) was going to be able to get a divorce. Life was not easy for RLS. Apart from being a chronic invalid he was also artistic, which was frowned upon by his oppressive Calvinist family in Scotland. As a young man he had finally escaped from their clutches and went to Paris where he spent his time writing and dallying with Fanny. When things got serious between them, they had to face up to two major problems: she was married, and his writing wasn't making enough money to support a wife. So they decided to make a combined effort to overcome both these problems simultaneously. She went back to California to try to persuade her husband to agree to a divorce and he went south to wander around the Highlands of France (as he called the Cévennes) to make a bit more money by writing a travel book (thus blazing a trail for Bill Bryson). As he said in his diary 'I travel for travel's sake. And to write about it afterwards if only the public will be so condescending as to read.'

Their efforts were crowned with success, though not immediately. The easy part was writing the book, which RLS did with his usual aplomb. He had a most vivid imagination and used to stay up all night in order to consign the results of his imagination to paper. Not that I'm saying he intentionally made up the contents of *Travels with a Donkey*, but you only have to read a dozen or so of the short stories he wrote when he was in Paris to be convinced that he couldn't help himself. He seems to be falling over himself in his haste to finish one story and get on with the next. So as soon as he was back in Paris, he rattled off *Travels with a Donkey in the Cévennes*. It was well received in England where the *Fortnightly Review* enthused 'His *Inland Voyage* [his first travel book: a very entertaining account of canoeing down the Meuse with a friend – no mention of donkeys] struck the keynote of his literary gamut; and the new volume of travel with which he now favours us, has the self-same happy ring, the self-same light and graceful touch, as if Mr Stevenson were rather a Frenchman born out of due place, than a Scotsman of the Scots.' He made a reasonable amount of money out of it. In fact if he were still alive, he would still be making money out of it today, as it continues to be one of his best-loved books and a steady seller.

However, the outcome of Fanny's attempt to obtain a divorce was less successful, so he had to go to America himself (where he fell ill yet again). In the end, however, the two lovers got their way. Once their romantic problems were all sorted out, they lived happily ever after. This involved gradually moving further and further south in an attempt to find a suitable climate for RLS's health. They went so far south that they finished up ten years later on the South Sea island of Samoa in the Pacific Ocean. By then RLS had written his most famous works: *Treasure Island*, *Kidnapped* and *Dr Jekyll and Mr Hyde*. Unfortunately, happily ever after for RLS and Fanny actually only lasted until he was forty-four, when he rather surprisingly died of a cerebral haemorrhage instead of the consumption which he had been fighting against ever since the cold and damp of the Scottish climate had first got to him in his early youth. In view of his chronic ill-health, dragging a donkey around the Cévennes at the beginning of the winter of 1878 was a very rash exploit, but he seemed physically none the worse for it – his sheepskin-lined sleeping bag and bottle of brandy must have done the trick.

The path that he took as he wandered around the mountains in giant zigzags, getting into arguments with locals and having trouble with his donkey, Modestine, now forms part of an official French footpath, the GR70, beautifully signposted and boasting frequent bed-and-breakfasts. It is popular with walkers, cyclists and donkeys – perhaps more popular with the people who pull donkeys than with the donkeys themselves. The Trail goes from north to south (rather like RLS's life's journey: from Scotland to the South Seas). He covered the 212km from Le Monastier to St Jean du Gard in twelve days, a thoroughly respectable time for a semi-invalid.

Being in the best of health, it took us four years. You may conclude from this that a consumptive disposition makes people walk faster or that, in these decadent days, even people who go to the gym most days or who go swimming three times per week have lost the capacity to walk rapidly anywhere. This is probably true, but it's more to do with the fact that, not waiting for a divorce and in no hurry at all, we did it in stages, for pleasure.

It was in 2000 that we decided to try walking the Stevenson Trail. On this first trip we started in the middle, just to dip in our toes, so to speak. Then the next year we went back to the beginning and started walking along it properly, sometimes just the two of us, sometimes with different people, as follows:

2000
May: A day trip for Hilary and me. This was when we discovered Gilles, our donkey-hirer.

2001
May: Five days, with two friends (Florence and Clive).
September: Five days, with two other friends (Véro and Dany).

October: A non-Stevenson Trail extra of five days' walking Gilles' donkeys down to their winter pastures.

2002
May: Five days – just Hilary and me again – by the end of which we were only a whisker away.

2003
February: Half a day – me, Véro, Dany and a new friend, Michèle – to finish it off (it really was only a short whisker).
May: Two days for Hilary and me on a donkeyless excursion to Notre Dame des Neiges and lunch at Pradelles.

Looking back, we had a much easier time than RLS, who had all sorts of difficulties. Apart from having to walk the whole thing all in one go, which must have been much more tiring, he was foreign at a time when Franco-British relations were rather strained. He wore funny boots, which you can see in Edinburgh, in the Writers' Museum (mind you, Hilary didn't do too well with her boots either to start with), and he didn't know the first thing about how to handle a donkey. In addition, part of his trip took him into the '*Bête du Gévaudan* country', where strangers at that time were treated with great suspicion due to the mysterious death of numerous young women a few years previously. To make matters worse, he had no mobile phone, no nice little red-and-white markers on the trees to indicate the way and no friendly bed-and-breakfasts where he could spend the night, have a shower and watch television (though we found some bed-and-breakfasts were friendlier than others). Unlike us, he couldn't get in the car and drive home when he'd had enough. He didn't even have an electric torch or a proper map (neither did we, but that was because we forgot them) and, what's more, he started out at the wrong time of year (September) when the weather begins to get really wet and cold and nasty and the nights are drawing in (it gets dark at 6pm).

We were very lucky, as we were able to do most of our trekking in May, which is a far superior time of year for walking the Trail. At this time of year the countryside is idyllic, bedecked with all manner of pretty flowers; and the long, languorous days give you the chance to wander off course and back on again without struggling along panic-stricken in pitch darkness, wondering if you will ever see hearth and home again.

Also, people on the Stevenson Trail are much more sociable nowadays than they were in Stevenson's time, if his book is anything to go by. We only met one person similar to the surly, miserable characters who seem to have peopled the Cévennes when Stevenson was around; the rest were helpful and charming. In a way, this is quite understandable as we were pretty good consumers of bed-and-breakfasts and evening meals, whereas Stevenson went in for self-catering in a big way, carrying legs of lamb with him and sleeping in woods. No wonder they were miffed.

Why did we do it? Silly question. A better one would be, why did we carry on year after year? I've no idea really but I'm so glad we did. Something to do with it being there, or perhaps because it was so enjoyable, particularly in retro-spect. That is why we decided to write this book. It gave us a chance to relive past pleasures – and past pain. We hope it will even encourage you to try it for yourselves. As an armchair guide, it can be read as light entertainment without you having to commit to putting on your walking boots. On the other hand, should you decide to do so, we have included a wealth of useful information – including the name of the guidebook that explains where to turn left, where to turn right, etc., and, most importantly, where to stop for supper.

Bon voyage!

UPS AND DOWNS

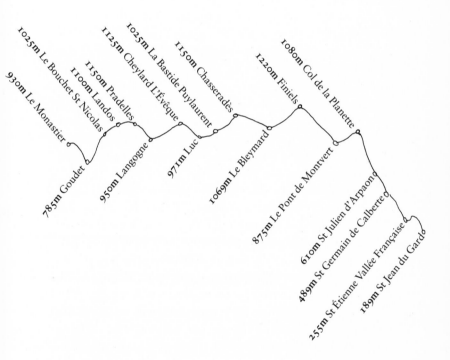

The Stevenson Trail in profile.

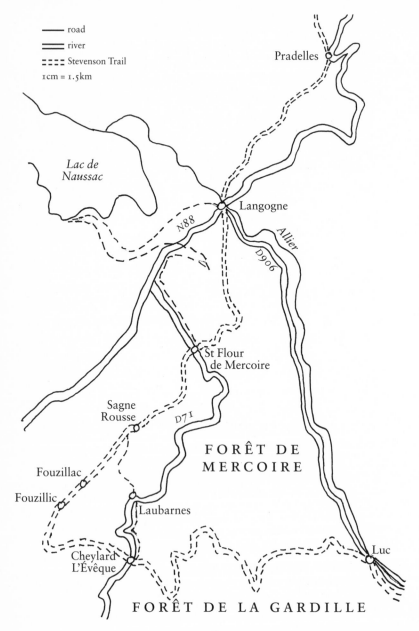

road
river
Stevenson Trail
1cm = 1.5km

Pradelles

Lac de Naussac

N88

Langogne

Allier

D906

St Flour de Mercoire

Sagne Rousse

D71

FORÊT DE MERCOIRE

Fouzillac

Fouzillic

Laubarnes

Luc

Cheylard L'Évêque

FORÊT DE LA GARDILLE

HOW NOT TO DO IT:
STARTING IN THE MIDDLE
Pradelles–Cheylard l'Évêque

In which Hilary finds quails' heads

As we manoeuvred our donkey through Langogne – it was market day, and our route lay along the packed high street, through the marketplace and a maze of reversing vans – Molly said 'It's a bit of an obscure thing to do, isn't it? To go for a walk with a donkey, just because someone else did 120 years ago.'

Travelling with a donkey had seemed rather appealing. The last time I was in France I'd seen a leaflet about the Trail, tracing the route Robert Louis Stevenson had taken with Modestine: called *En Cévennes avec un âne*, it had shown a sweet picture of a toddler asleep between the donkey's ears. Then Molly, who had lived in France for twenty-five years, told me about the Stevenson Trail. There were, she said, donkey bed-and-breakfasts where traveller and donkey could put up for the night. I was enthused. (It's true that I did think at that stage that the donkey would be transporting us, as well as our belongings.)

We started out from Pradelles, skipping the first stage from Le Monastier (I'd read somewhere that this was the least interesting part). We'd found a colourful map on the Internet (it was practically our only preparation, apart from my re-reading *Travels with a Donkey* on Eurostar) and the photos of medieval Pradelles made it look pretty.

So it was. But as we drove carefully through the village on its Cévennes hilltop, we couldn't see any sign of donkeys. Tired and hungry, we made for the bar in the centre to enquire. As we parked, a faded yellow ex-postal van, the words *La Poste* still visible on its side, drew up in the village square. In the back was a donkey.

A man with immense moustache and checked shirt, his glasses dangling from a cord round his neck, got out from behind the driving wheel, followed us into the bar, whisked behind the counter, tucked a tea towel round his waist and within minutes was cooking us a fine steak and chips. It was Gilles Romand, our donkey-hirer. The bar, the Brasserie du Musée, was another of his businesses. He also owned the stone-walled, sprucely pine-timbered *gîte d'étape*, where we were to spend the night, and the rather jolly Musée du Cheval, with its animated Stevenson display, round the corner. 'I bet he's mayor as well,' I muttered to Molly. (He wasn't – but he had been.)

Later that evening we met Noisette, who was to be our companion on the Stevenson Trail. She was the donkey in the van. Gilles led her out into a field by the museum, where two young donkeys, Loustic and Lola, eagerly trotted over to greet her. Noisette kicked her heels up at them in a most unfriendly manner.

'She likes to be alone,' said Gilles. That didn't bode too well. But he also said reassuringly that she was '*calme*', '*gentille*' and '*sage*'. His wife added quietly later that she was '*maligne*' ('cunning'). However, she was, importantly, *calme* when we introduced her to Whiskey, Molly's young Labrador, who, though a shining graduate of dog obedience classes, had not met a donkey before and was displaying vociferous disapproval. Noisette flapped her ears a little but took no more notice of him.

The next morning, Gilles helped us fill the leather panniers, lent us his copy of the guidebook, *Le Chemin de Stevenson* (it hadn't taken him long to realise how hopelessly equipped we were) and gave us a quick lesson in donkey management.

'Stevenson must have had a job,' he added. 'You need two people with a donkey, one to push and one to pull.'

With a final exhortation to fill our bottles from the one of the many fountains (we forgot, and were to deeply regret that later) he waved us off down the hill along the road that went through an arch under the twelfth-century church, past the cemetery on the left and then – where? There were two paths directly opposite. The guidebook did not clarify which one. We were only on the verge of Pradelles and already on the verge of being lost.

We took the more attractive path, which luckily, it was soon obvious, was the right one. Two solid brown carthorses, tossing glamorous blond manes like ageing film stars, came to inspect our little procession as we marched with some satisfaction towards Langogne between fields blazing with golden broom. It was not exactly quiet – the sound of skylarks and cacophony of crickets saw to that – but it was deeply rural and peaceful. Until we reached Langogne.

Noisette took that seething maelstrom in her stride, disregarding the excitement of buying and selling and the genial shouts of market visitors who had spotted us: 'Bring the donkey into the bar, his brother's already having a drink in here.' But we were relieved to reach a high-hedged grassy lane where we had lunch. While Molly did a little Qigong – knees slightly bent, eyes closed – I looked to see what RLS had said of our next destination, Cheylard l'Évêque: 'A man, I was told, should walk there in an hour and a half; and I thought it scarce too ambitious that a man encumbered with a donkey might cover the same distance in four hours.'

Our spirits rose. Four hours was nothing. (Had I remembered the next bit, I might have been less cheerful: RLS didn't actually make it that day.) But there was a difference that we hadn't appreciated: RLS had the measure of his donkey by this point. We hadn't. And we had not made allowances for that.

Hilary getting lost with Noisette near Langogne.

We set off purposefully, or would have done had it not been for Noisette, whose customary pace, it was astonishing to remark, was slower than mine. She took precious little notice of the carrots we had brought. Gilles was right – she really did have to be pushed.

When we came to a sign proclaiming '*une modification*' to the Stevenson Trail we decided, sensibly, to stick to the guidebook and, after scurrying across the N88 (which after half a day on these lanes seemed like a motorway), experienced that glow of achievement derived from reading a map correctly when we found the 'muddy lane' mentioned in the book through a farmyard full of chicks scattering, dogs yapping. But then we were brought up short by another large sign, '*Propriété Privée*,' and a fence across the path. So that's why there was '*une modification*'. Why, we muttered in a resigned sort of way, did they not add '*obligatoire*' or '*nécessaire*'?

We stopped for a few minutes while I changed my boots for sandals; my ill-prepared state had extended as far as borrowing my daughter's boots – after all, what difference would a half-size make? A lot, as I had now found out. Then we patiently retraced our steps, scurried across the N88 again and followed the distinctive red-and-white signs that denoted an official footpath in the opposite direction alongside a golf course, secure in the knowledge that these were the markings of the Trail. By now Noisette was definitely loitering. We were reduced to smacking her on the rump with the guidebook, at which she would quicken her pace for a step or two and then lapse into her customary dawdle, as though utterly uninterested in any destination.

It was, we remarked to each other, a very long golf course, and here was a cattle grid – curious to have one of those on a trail used by donkeys. We carefully undid the barbed-wire-and-paling fence next to it to lead Noisette through, and walked a little further. Look, here we were at the lake at last.

The lake? What were we doing at the lake? We'd last seen it behind us near Pradelles. We had, yet again, gone wrong.

We painstakingly dismantled and reassembled the barbed-wire-and-paling fence again and retraced our steps back to the N88, which, by this stage, at least had the virtue of familiarity. We gave up reading the guidebook and trudged up the N88, grimly towing Noisette along the verge as cars thundered past. After a daunting fifteen minutes, we were back on course and stopped to rest. (It was at this point that I must have sat in something that excited Whiskey hugely. Eagerly he kept bounding over to me, sniffing at my trousers, and licking me lasciviously. For the rest of the day, I had to put up with the fact that, apart from everything else, I was the victim of a dog's lust.)

We cheered ourselves with the thought that we would soon be at St Flour de Mercoire and would reward ourselves with beer. We fantasised about foaming glasses and cool liquid. We were even prepared to enjoy the scenery again, which was terrific throughout the day. Because winter lingers late in the mountains, spring arrives all at once with a clamour: fields of narcissi like stars, banks of forget-me-nots, tiny yellow and cream wild pansies, campions, violets, daisies, poppies, buttercups and cowslips, even occasional orchids spread before us and stretched away in fields beside us. And everywhere was the bright brilliance of broom.

But we did not get our beer. Shockingly, St Flour had no bar. Nor even a shop. The only sign of life was a pair of dogs, dashing and snapping at Whiskey. When they were called off by their owner, our first human contact for a while, we were at least able to ask to have our water bottles replenished: a poor substitute, but we were so parched by then that we were grateful even for that. We plodded on and up towards Sagne Rousse by a steep path through forests, with glades where – in a parallel universe, unencumbered by a recalcitrant donkey – we would have liked to linger. But it was getting late. At last there were signs of civilisation in the form of dappled cows grazing in a grove of gnarled old pine trees, and then a *menhir Stevenson*, an inscribed lump of rock blessedly marking the route.

It was 6pm and the sun was slipping behind the hills, so we decided to cheat again and walk along a road – at least we knew it went to Cheylard l'Évêque. Three cyclists passed, asking helpfully if we were lost. For once we knew we weren't. But this was when Noisette decided to demonstrate her *maligne* side. At any moment when our attention wandered – to look at the map, to admire the flowers – she was off into the ditch, browsing as though her life depended on it. Each time it took both of us pulling at the leading rein to dislodge her.

But there at last at Laubarnes – where a gleaming black stallion careered over to examine us more closely, indulging in a bit of showy rearing up – we could see Cheylard l'Évêque in the valley below, overlooked by its chapel-shrine to St Mary. 'Candidly, it seemed little worthy of all this searching', RLS had written. It looked pretty good to us. Even if, we realised as we strode down the precipitous hairpin road, we would have to go uphill to continue the Trail tomorrow.

Soon at the Refuge du Moure, run by M. and Mme. Simonet, we were all being catered for: Whiskey was directed to a kennel, Noisette to a field following M. Simonet with his blue plastic bucket of oats (she had suddenly become rather jaunty) and we to a room beneath the eaves. Once inside, however, we had to take off our boots and put on pairs of checked slippers from a rack in the hall: M. Simonet was most particular about that. In the dining room, where there were shelves of home-made jams – melon, banana and rhubarb, peach, each with its own little pleated paper hat – we joined the cyclists who had passed us earlier for a four-course meal, starring quails. (Disconcertingly, as I discovered when I put my glasses on, their heads were still attached; Molly's even had its little beak open.)

But we were in no mood for fine food. Our bodies ached utterly. Our feet too. (Molly's ancient boots, purchased in student days, had almost given out before we had started. And I was still suffering from having foolishly borrowed my daughter's boots.) By my reckoning we had walked nearer 30km than the 20km predicted. Rain was forecast for the next day and I had just discovered that my smug self-congrat-ulation at bringing two sets of waterproofs was misplaced – one waterproof jacket was still on the bed at home. Molly, after examining the map and calculating the distance and contours of the next day's journey to the Trappist monastery of Notre Dame des Neiges, was miserable. We went to bed very early and in deep gloom.

Early the next morning, Molly went to visit Whiskey in his kennel and reappeared in the bedroom with her face wreathed in smiles. 'Would you be *very* disappointed if I told you that we couldn't carry on, and we had to go back?' It seemed too good to be true. Whiskey, unused to walking along roads, had sore paws. There was, it seemed, no alterna-tive. We might – despite our suffering feet – be able to walk, but Whiskey certainly couldn't.

Shrugging off the disapproval of M. Simonet – he made it clear that he thought us utterly feeble – we phoned Gilles, who cheerfully came to fetch us. Later that morning we saw, for the first time, Noisette trotting – into the van; she had clearly had enough too. But something strange happened on the way back (which took a mere half hour, by the way). By the time we were ensconced in the Brasserie du Musée and drinking cups of hot chocolate, Molly had made a decision: 'I am absolutely consumed with a desire to come back next year and do it properly.' And so it was fixed. Gilles booked us in for six days. Next time, he said, he would give us a donkey with a bit of 'oomph'. And we would buy the new edition of the guidebook.

TIPS FOR THE FUTURE

In which Hilary remembers the things not to forget

1. Buy up-to-date guidebook
2. Pack both waterproof jackets
3. Consult up-to-date map beforehand
4. Bring said up-to-date map on trip
5. Learn footpath identification code
6. Take notice of signs on the route
7. Take boots of the correct size
8. Harden the dog's feet before the expedition
9. Line rucksacks with bin bags
10. Pack riding gloves (to save delicate hands) in an accessible place
11. Take large quantities of packed lunch (or legs of lamb) to compensate for lack of bars/shops
12. Fill water bottles when advised
13. Do not wear glasses to eat quails
14. Learn French

A JOURNEY THROUGH HISTORY –
OF THE CÉVENNES AND THE
STEVENSON TRAIL (1100–1994)

In which Molly pots some history

The history of the Cévennes has been marked by bloody-minded-
ness dating from the beginning of time. Cévennes dwellers didn't
accept the Romans, they didn't accept Christianity (they preferred
the Visigoths) and they didn't accept the Catholic Church (they
preferred first the Vaudois, then the Cathars and later Calvin and
the Huguenots). So far they have not yet founded an Independence
Movement but I'm sure they would have done if they'd been living
on an island or at one end of France and not in the middle.

But why should Cévennes dwellers be so difficult? Can it be
chronic indigestion due to too much chestnut bread, which used
to make up their staple diet? Eating the wrong types of mushroom? Can it be too much rain? Being cut off in the winter? (Until
very recently they used to have to store the body of anyone who
died in the winter on the roof of the house – nice and cold and out
of the reach of scavengers – until they could get the pastor around
to bury it properly when the thaw set in.) And why are current
Cévennes dwellers nowadays mostly charming? Whatever the
answer to all these questions, the fact still remains that a lot of
persecution and suffering and war and pillaging and murder went
on in the Cévennes over the 700 years before Stevenson went
along his Trail, to say nothing of a bit of serial killing and/or were-
wolfing. No wonder their nerves were on edge.

Historical fact no. 1: In 1175, Pierre Valdes, a rich merchant
from Lyons, was converted to humility and poverty and a desire
to follow the original scriptures. Like all the newly converted he
went around loudly sharing these discoveries with all and

sundry. This was very badly received by the Catholic Church but seized upon with enthusiasm by Cévennes dwellers. In 1184 followers of Valdes (aka the Vaudois) were excommunicated lock, stock and barrel, but they carried on all the same and in 1532 they officially joined the Protestant Reform Movement which was sweeping through Europe. Meanwhile the Cévennes (along with the whole of the South of France) had been ravaged by the Great Plague and then the Hundred Years War.

Historical fact no. 2: In 1572, numerous Calvinist chiefs were massacred on St Bartholomew's Day (24 August) by the official French (Catholic) army which was getting very bored with being resisted on a constant basis. Unfortunately, although it must have seemed a good idea at the time, it only caused more violence in the shape of reprisals from Calvinists.

Historical fact no. 3: In 1579, an enterprising chap called Captain Merle dismantled the cathedral at Mende (just off the Stevenson Trail) stone by stone, because it was Catholic. Dismantling the cathedral was not as easy as it sounds and it caused him to become irritable and unpleasant with his prisoners (e.g. hanging clergymen upside down over open fires until they paid ransoms). He and his army spread terror for years. In fact, when he had finished, not only was the cathedral demolished but also numerous towns, castles and churches over a wide area.

Historical fact no. 4: In 1598, Good King Henry (Henri IV) – who was a nice, cuddly person and who wished all French people to be able to have a good meal at least once a week – tried to calm things down by issuing the Edict of Nantes which gave freedom to worship and legitimacy to Protestants.

Historical fact no. 5: On learning that, in England, Charles II had been decapitated by Cromwell (1649), Louis XIV, Henri IV's grandson, concluded that it was dangerous to be lenient to Protestants so he started issuing measures to reduce their freedom. As he had hoped, this caused a massive exodus of Protestants. In the 1660s and 1670s thousands of them (mainly the prosperous middle classes, merchants and artisans who could afford to travel) moved out to Switzerland and parts of Germany, where they joined up with local Vaudois (hence the name of the Swiss canton called the Vaud). This marked the beginning of the depopulation of the Cévennes. To make matters worse for the remaining Cévennes dwellers, Louis then revoked the Edict of Nantes in 1685, outlawing all Protestants in any shape or form and giving Royal and Catholic troops the go-ahead to torture, imprison and otherwise oppress anyone who was thought to be Protestant. Which they did.

Historical fact no. 6: This brings us to Le Pont de Montvert (on the Stevenson Trail). In 1702 there was a very bloody battle when a local boy called Esprit Séguier led an uprising to free the prisoners of the Catholic Abbé du Chayla and killed the Abbot in the process. Séguier was burned at the stake as a heretic in August of the same year and thus the war of the Camisards began.

Historical fact no. 7: Things then went from bad to worse with battles, skirmishes, rebellions, murders, pillagings and razings-to-the-ground of villages, etc. Finally, in 1787, Louis XVI signed an Edict of Tolerance allowing Protestants to worship, marry, bury their dead and all the other things that fully paid-up members of society are allowed to do.

Historical fact no. 8: '*Ouf!*' went the Cévennes dwellers. 'Thank goodness that's over.' But it wasn't, because the next thing to happen was the French Revolution which started in 1789 and then, as if that wasn't enough, from 1794 onwards, the *Bête du Gévaudan* began to rampage around. Perhaps the *bête* was a wolf or perhaps it wasn't, but it went round killing and ripping the throats out of young women and terrorised the area. It was never really proved who or what was behind it but some thirty women were killed in this region over the next five years. At this point, most of the people who were still alive packed their bags and went, leaving only those who couldn't afford to leave (and lovers of chestnut bread) living in the area.

Historical fact no. 9: In 1878, Stevenson came along and was received with dubious enthusiasm when he went around knocking on doors in the middle of stormy nights. It is doubtful if he would be better received today, particularly in remote country areas with no telephone. Personally, I wouldn't take kindly to anyone banging on my door in the middle of the night and shouting abuse in a foreign language.

Historical fact no. 10: In 1994, Stevenson was forgiven for his uncouth behaviour and the *Association 'Sur le Chemin de Robert Louis Stevenson'* was founded to promote the Stevenson Trail. Association members run *gîtes*, hotels, restaurants and campsites, hire out donkeys and provide warm welcomes to visitors. The natural beauty of the Cévennes has done the rest and the Trail is a success, visited by tourists and Stevenson-lovers from around the world.

In fact, as you may have gathered, tourists represent the first massive influx of people to come to the Cévennes without the avowed intent of killing everyone in their way and feeling totally justified in doing so. Perhaps that's why people in the Cévennes are much more charming nowadays than they were when Stevenson was there.

The Stevenson Trail crossing Gévaudan country.

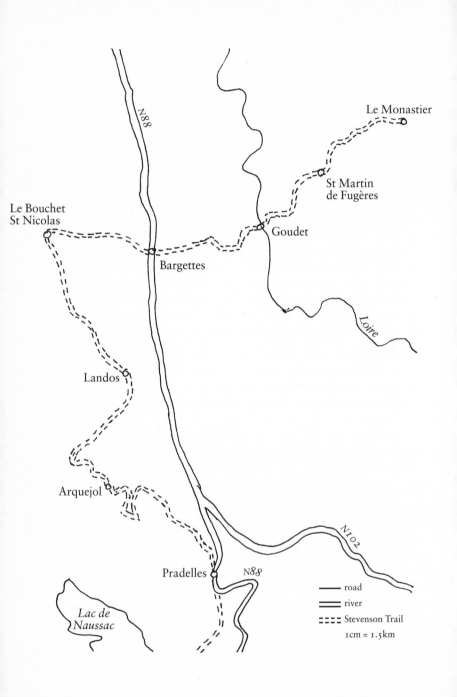

Le Monastier

St Martin
de Fugères

N88

Goudet

Le Bouchet
St Nicolas

Bargettes

Loire

Landos

Arquejol

N102

Pradelles

N88

Lac de
Naussac

road

river

Stevenson Trail

1cm = 1.5km

STARTING PROPERLY:
FROM THE BEGINNING
Le Monastier–Pradelles

In which Hilary is fascinated by a farmer

This time on the Trail, things would be different. We'd be better prepared for a start. And we would have companions. We'd had such a good time on our first trip (seemed to be our curious line of thinking, now months distant from that ordeal) that we would invite others to share the experience.

So Molly invited Clive, a retired diplomat living in Languedoc (his last posting: the British consulate in Bordeaux). It was from him that Molly had first heard about the Stevenson Trail. Then there was her friend from work, Florence, who knew about horses. It seemed an excellent qualification for helping us do the Stevenson Trail properly.

And we would begin at the beginning: Le Monastier, where RLS had conceived his expedition, bought his donkey and – by trial and error – assembled his odd assortment of equipment. By contrast, we were returning to Pradelles to hire ours from Gilles Romand, owner of twelve donkeys and expert on all things asinine.

Gilles was in the kitchen of the Brasserie du Musée when Molly, Florence and I arrived on the eve of our expedition. He briefly appeared to announce that he wasn't asking us what we wanted for dinner. He was going to give us what he decided to cook. This turned out to be green salad with Puy lentils, *confit de porc* with boiled potatoes, sitting in an actually rather tasty pool of fat (a signature dish, Molly and I later decided), plus *fromage blanc*, bread and butter pudding with cream and *crème anglaise* – all accompanied with copious quantities of red wine. In our satiated state it seemed that Gilles was expert on all things culinary too.

The first sign of any problem was after our first night in the *gîte*. I slept well. Poor Florence didn't. Someone was snoring, she said, looking at me and sighing in a resigned sort of way.

We were all a bit sluggish but Gilles whisked us into activity, hurrying us down to the field outside the village to collect our donkey. This year we were having Jeep. The name was a good omen – he would surely have more 'oomph' than Noisette. With Jeep installed in the back of Gilles' new white van, and the three of us plus Whiskey squashed into the front seat alongside Gilles, we belted over to Le Monastier, past acres of lentil fields. It took us forty-five minutes. It would take us three days to get back as far as Pradelles. Not for the first time did I ponder the pointlessness of this exercise.

Gilles pulled up flamboyantly in the centre of the main square to unload donkey, us and all our belongings in their numerous black plastic bags and little rucksacks and straw baskets. A brief burst of packing activity ensued as these were all stowed and re-stowed in the leather panniers, strapped across the wooden frame (*bât*), dangling from the straps, or – as with Whiskey's drinking bowl – perched on top. All was donkey-shape and ready to go when Clive and his wife Auriol arrived in their BMW. Clive would accompany us for two days; Auriol, a committed driver rather than a walker, would meet us that evening at Goudet.

Le Monastier, stolidly medieval and somnolent, is perhaps rather less exciting than when RLS stayed there. He too, however, was lamenting the passing of a previously much more exciting time in its prosperous past: 'From week's end to week's end it was one continuous gala in Monastier; people spent the day in the wine-shops, and the drum or the bagpipes led on the *bourrées* up to ten a night. Now these dancing days are over.' But there were still fifty wine-shops in his day and chatty lace-makers who worked outside. 'The women sit in the streets by groups of five or six; and the noise of the bobbins is audible from one group to another. They wear gaudy shawls, white caps with a gay ribbon about the head, and sometimes a black felt brigand hat above the cap; and so they give the street colour and brightness and a foreign air.' They have gone and it is Le Monastier's loss. But we were not inclined to linger to investigate any compensating finer points. We wanted to hit the Trail. At least we knew this time that we left town on the right route: we passed the new-looking stone plaque which marks the spot where RLS – apparently – started: '*Ici partit le 22 Septembre 1878 Robert Louis Stevenson pour son voyage à travers les Cévennes avec l'âne.*'

Our *âne* this year was indeed, as promised, more energetic than Noisette. No pushing required; no pulling. Phlegmatically, even jauntily, accepting his lot, he led the small procession. But there was one snag. Jeep, we'd been warned in advance, didn't like dogs. For a party which had a dog as a founder member, this was to prove a bit of a disadvantage.

We followed faithfully in the footsteps of Stevenson, consulting guidebook (an up-to-date edition this time) in one hand and, to start with at least, *Travels with a Donkey* in the other. Thus we found that instead of the ford over the Gazielle, tiny tributary of the Loire, there is now a bridge, but after crossing that we climbed up into the pine forests along what must have been the exact track RLS had used. Alas, I couldn't entirely capture his spirit. He was, by his account, venturing into wild country with only a rough idea of direction along tracks which, on occasion, diverged three or four different ways with no clue as the right one. We, on the other hand, were constantly guided by the red-and-white markings of the *Grandes Randonnées*, walking within safe boundaries, as along an unroofed corridor with unseen walls. We were following a step-by-step guidebook. It was hard to imagine ourselves into the proper sense of adventure that he must have had.

But we could identify with his sense of victimisation. The day had started in suitably spring-like fashion, with blackbirds singing furiously. But by the time we had reached the first crossroads on the plateau, it was raining. I didn't mind. I felt smug. This year, my boots were my own, and they appeared to be entirely leak-free. I'd brought my waterproofs with me. I'd remembered to protect my belongings with a black bin bag.

Clive, less well prepared, made do with a second cagoule that Florence had efficiently brought along. It was too small but, putting the hood over his head, he spread it over his shoulders like a cape, which protected him from the worst. The plastic bags lining Molly's boots seemed to be doing the trick for her. We all remained stoically cheerful. Then stoically silent. Our shared vocal appreciation of the mountain ranges and fields of orchids subsided. We ate our lunch standing under a tree, with the rain pattering through the branches. Then we sheltered under the overhanging eaves of a barn in St Martin de Figuères during a thunderstorm. That was the first thunderstorm. We tramped on through the second. And the third. That one was accompanied by hail. By mid-afternoon, my smugness had worn off. I was now walking in two self-contained puddles. I'd remembered that the small rucksack on my back was not lined with a bin bag – so my one and only jumper was wringing wet, my notebook was sodden and a wodge of stamps thoughtfully purchased in advance, was now unfit for any purpose without some glue (which I had failed to include in my list of necessities, comprehensive though it was compared to last year's feeble effort).

But towards the end of the day, the sky lightened at last. As we took the narrow dry-stone-walled track down to Goudet, threading our way through a mass of golden broom, a sudden sunny view of the riverside village overlooked by its castle ruins, all gap-toothed, appeared. Our spirits lifted.

Near the bottom we met two riders. The horses looked sleek and well-cared-for. The riders looked wild. The man had long hair, a Zapata moustache and a leather wide-brimmed hat. The woman's grey hair flowed over the shoulders of her great cape. With them were three dogs, the first with only one eye, each with a bell on its collar. They were travelling the Camino de Santiago de Compostela, which seemed unbelievably exotic to us, but for their part they were more interested in our little cavalcade, capturing it on film for their own records.

At the Hôtel de la Loire, beside the youthful river, the donkey was led away to a field and we were led to our bedrooms. That is the delightful thing about most donkey bed-and-breakfasts: at the end of a day on the Trail, someone takes the donkey away and deals with it, leaving the humans to have hot baths, eat good food and return to a human state of mind.

Unfortunately, this often encompasses discussion of the state of the real world, easily and happily forgotten when battling with the elements outside on the Trail. Over the rich *boeuf bourguignon* that evening, conversation ranged from robbery in France (having left my passport and wallet in Florence's car in Pradelles I was dismayed as the talk turned to the apparently common occurrence of cars being stolen, dismantled and emptied of contents while owners were away for ten minutes) to experiences in the diplomatic service and social practices in other parts of the world ('There was no thieving in the Congo. Thieves were killed.').

The Hôtel de la Loire, I was sure, must have been the hotel where RLS had lunched, after which he wrote about admiring the portrait of his host's nephew, 'Professor of Fencing and Champion of the two Americas'. But I couldn't find the picture before we left the next morning to tackle the hill out of Goudet, described by RLS as 'interminable'. Perhaps he had eaten his lunch too quickly. Perhaps he had not had a long enough rest. We didn't find it so bad: the path was precipitous but within minutes we were gratifyingly on a level with the castle on the next hill, and then, quite soon, high above it. The track rose and twisted between lentil fields. '*Les lentilles vertes du Puy,*' said a sign on a farm building, '*vente à la ferme.*'

At Montagnac we found ourselves in sunshine, the creamy cloud now below us, roosting in the valley, but the path onwards lay along a road. Cars sped along, their drivers casting the occasional curious glance but not reducing their speed at all. It felt like quite an achievement when we made it, safely and intact, to a pretty lane between hedges, all grassy underfoot and sprayed with wild flowers – cowslips, narcissi, forget-me-nots. Molly picked some to adorn our room that night.

We had lunch here, but could not dawdle, for Clive had arranged an assignation with Auriol. What took us several

Hilary admiring Goudet in the valley and Château de Beaufort beyond.

hours to do, she could cover in a few minutes in the elegant silver BMW with cream leather seats. This part of the country was sparsely populated, with few villages or diversions: she was at a loose end and already waiting for us at Bargettes. It was mildly unsettling, reminding us of the world outside the Trail. But then we were off again, into the world between roads.

Our destination that night was Le Bouchet St Nicolas. There Clive and Auriol were to leave us, departing many miles south to an excellent restaurant they knew of in Florac – a village also on the Stevenson Trail, but an unbelievably far goal from our foot- and hoof-bound point of view. At Le Bouchet St Nicolas RLS had stayed at an *auberge*, 'the least pretentious I have ever visited' with its meal of 'hard fish and omelette'. Our quarters, a restaurant with rooms, were a little more distinguished.

The only negative aspect was that the donkey's quarters were in Mme. Josette's field at the other end of the village. Grudgingly, we trudged along the road leading the donkey, pausing to allow the passage of a herd of brown and white cows, mild and curious about Jeep (though the combined tonnage of successive groups of four or five stopping to turn towards us, leaning over in speculative unison, was a bit alarming). We led Jeep into a large field with other donkeys, where he kicked his heels up in glee and galloped about, pausing occasionally to rip mouthfuls of grass from the ground. At last we could turn our attention to our own supper. The only thing we were certain of, after our day's ramblings past local crops, was that it would contain lentils.

But it turned out to be a long wait. It was Ascension Day and on our arrival in late afternoon the restaurant was still packed with first communion celebrations: it was full of young girls in white dresses and high spirits, streamers and decorations and piles of profiteroles in pyramids or shaped like houses.

Whenever we were at the height of our exertions, bent over against rain or struggling up hills, we would fantasise about all sorts of pleasures. A good meal was always top of the list. But sometimes when it comes to it, the metabolism snaps into rebellion and fine food turns out to be the very last thing it wants, such is the perversity of human nature. This was one such occasion. It was partly because the meal started late, but mainly because the meal itself took so long. The *patronne* – a slender, size 6 sort of person with dyed red hair and a loud, clear way of speaking – was very hospitable and talked to everyone in the restaurant. Individually. In turn.

She also gave a detailed account of each course of the meal, every single ingredient of which was provided by a *producteur local*. It was, despite our exhaustion, pretty sensational. We started with aperitifs – home-made gentian wine, a great rarity, made from the root of the plant, and smelling faintly of horseradish. It set the tone for the elaborate meal crammed full of regional goodies. On our table were placed three great bowls of green salad, mixed with chicken livers and chunks of toasted *brioche*. The main course consisted of thin slices of veal with mashed parsnip and Puy lentils baked in cream and shreds of bacon. There followed a wide selection of cheeses, each described with great care by the *patronne*.

By this time we were flagging, alternating between lassitude and hysterical hilarity. Anyone with any sense would have gone to bed. But our tenacity – and respect for dessert courses – was greater than that. We were determined to find out what the pudding was. It was home-made strawberry ice cream, accompanied by tiny wild strawberries and almond biscuits. An hour earlier, we would have been ecstatic. Now we were desperate. We stuffed it down and rushed off to bed.

But sleeping was turning out to be a bone of contention. Apparently Molly yelped in the night, Whiskey panted, lapped water and licked himself frenziedly, and I 'breathed very loudly', according to Florence the next day. I was inclined to think that the problem lay more in Florence's acute hearing.

There was another difficulty. Florence owned a horse. She was also an organiser. Put the two together and, not surprisingly, it was Florence who took daily charge of harnessing and handling the donkey. Gradually, Molly and I were being dislocated from one of the objects of the expedition.

She felt responsible for Jeep's welfare. 'Is it safe for Jeep?' she would ask anxiously, as Molly and I crossed an old grassy stone bridge or clambered up a steep path. And she was scrupulous about keeping Jeep and Whiskey apart. Donkey–dog relations were not good: Jeep's intolerance of dogs had been demonstrated when he had kicked out at a passing stray at Le Bouchet St Nicolas. Though protective of Whiskey, Molly was nevertheless irritated when instructed to walk behind. 'I'm beginning to feel like a leper,' she grumbled. Without Clive to accompany either donkey-handler or dog-walker, the expedition became divided – it was no longer a cavalcade. Part of the pleasure was conviviality, conversation

Hilary, Florence and Jeep toiling towards Le Bouchet St Nicolas.

and solidarity in the teeth of adversity. Spread out as we were, taking turns with donkey or dog, this was impossible.

The first stage of the next day's journey, along a broad dirt road to Landos was very flat (that much was appreciated) and very dull, particularly when we couldn't talk to each other. Our only pleasure was in covering the distance in the allotted time in the guidebook, a rare achievement, especially since we had a donkey to deal with too.

At Landos, we negotiated our way past an elderly asthmatic dog with a very small bark – Whiskey was suitably disdainful – to the Bar de la Bascule in the market square. We were checking out lampposts and the wrought-iron hooks for the hanging baskets when the owner came out of the bar, moved a flower pot and pointed out a hitching ring – just right for Jeep.

The half-dozen people inside were all fascinated by us. We were cross-examined. Where were we going? Did we have a guide? Were we really doing it all alone? Every now and again, Jeep on the other side of the window would add his voice to the discussion and bray loudly, his nostrils widening and flaring, his upper and lower lips curved back, baring his large teeth. The villagers were even more fascinated by that. Curiously, right in the middle of the Stevenson Trail, it was as though they never saw donkeys. When we left, they waved us off like old friends.

We stopped quite soon again – for food, of course – eating our lunch on a pretty hillside where we could watch an old man, very bent, very slowly ushering a herd of goats into a meadow. Following the principle that the family that eats together stays together, we weren't doing badly. We were certainly all retaining and sharing a healthy common interest in food.

In the post-prandial glow, the afternoon passed pleasantly enough. The air was balmy and scented, the sun warm. As the path meandered gently up to a railway line, past a medieval stone cross, we took off our waterproof jackets, then our jumpers, and were striding along at unaccustomed speed when, with barely a moment's notice, rain came cascading down and we were scrambling for our waterproofs again. By the next corner, my 'shower-resistant' trousers were sticking wetly to my legs. Molly had had the sense to keep her waterproof trousers on. But then she had to put up with boots that leaked immoderately.

The sun had come out again by the time we arrived at Arquejol, at an exciting time – coinciding with the arrival of the *épicerie* van and a roaming pack of dogs. The van raced in, horn blaring to announce its arrival. A procession of old ladies, all wearing calf-length blue patterned cover-all aprons, made their way towards the van, as a stooped old man, quick on the scene, hobbled away with two long loaves. Florence and Molly, united for once, were preoccupied with the dogs. Five or six were approaching from different directions, like a platoon using a pincer movement, and heralding their arrival with a dissonant chorus of barks. But it was all just for show: Jeep and Whiskey, under the firm control of their guardians, remained calm and our little band survived unscathed. As we headed towards the Arquejol viaduct we returned to our solitary, spread-out musings. Occasionally we stopped together to stand and stare: at a corner field spiked thickly all over with orchids, purple and pink and cream; or a bravura avian display as in a garden at La Narse – a flock of guinea fowl moving away from the path in dignified perfect step with each other; a pair of white chickens running, side by side, awkward, ungainly; and, while the geese were raising their necks to look at us as though on tiptoe, the ducks at the back were marching off in single file.

Even a farmer towing a water tank into a field seemed fascinating, when watching his patient manoeuvres would put off the moment of steep ascent. Clambering up eventually to rejoin Florence and Jeep, I offered to take over Jeep duty and, deep in concentration on that task, it was startling to find myself suddenly in a utopian landscape. We were on a plateau, a mountain meadow. It was like a Swiss pasture, full of long seeded grasses suffused with more flowers than we'd ever seen: lady's smock, narcissi, forget-me-nots, speedwell, buttercups. On one side there were thickly ranked pine trees; on the other, a far-off range of mountains; above, the blue sky was scattered with white clouds out of a Constable painting. It was a sublime pastoral scene.

But eventually we had to move. Our path lay under the pine trees. Quite suddenly, as we entered the Bois des Chatourneyres, we were pricked into keen awareness that the air – not exactly noisy before – was absolutely still and hushed. Silent ourselves, we turned down a rugged rocky path which was more like the bed of a river – muddled, strewn about with debris. It was hard to see where the actual path lay. As the then-leader of Jeep, I felt charged with responsibility. But selecting the route was a joint enterprise, as Jeep stepped delicately round boulders, over rivulets, round fallen branches and through thick mud. (My boots, I realised later, were glinting, covered with tiny flecks of gold – or was it fool's gold? Generations ago, there was panning for gold in the Cévennes, so perhaps it was the real thing.) Absorbed and vigilant, I was keenly aware of Jeep picking his way, so sure-footed. My respect rose: this was no mere pack animal. I felt a rare sense of being in tune – with Jeep and with the environment.

We were then out in the open again, on the road leading to Pradelles, starting point of our expeditions and centre of our donkey universe. I felt there should have been banners and flag-waving, perhaps even palms strewn before our feet – it seemed we had achieved so much. But we were, as usual, alone on our road.

Proud, exhausted and united in common purpose – well, that's how it seemed to me at that time – we arrived back at the *gîte*. We unloaded the panniers, lifted the *bât* off the donkey's back and brought everything up to the dormitory. But Florence, in a great wordless rush, then threw off her waterproofs and

A street in Pradelles.

changed her clothes. She was, she announced, taking the donkey back to Gilles. She was concerned about a bare patch rubbed clear of fur that she had found on Jeep's left shoulder.

When she returned half an hour later, she was agitated, talking so fast that I couldn't catch it all, but her upset, her exasperation, was clear. Then, in English for my benefit, she said she was sad and hungry, no not hungry, *angry*, with us all for mistreating the donkey. Gilles had said that it was better to rest Jeep, she reported, to allow the bare patch caused by the pannier to recover. She felt it personally, as a chastisement. The responsibility (self-imposed) of the last few days had suddenly become all too much for Florence. And she drew us in too. We were all too tired, she said. We should stop the expedition now.

Molly sat on the chair between the bunks, not arguing but with a certain stony look in her eye. She didn't like assumptions and decisions being made for her by someone else – that *she* was tired and that *we* should stop at Pradelles. There was a tension between Florence and Molly that I didn't have to be fluent in French to pick up on.

Florence showered and emerged calmer. She backtracked a bit. We went to the brasserie for a restorative meal. Kir for all, on the house, mellowed us a little, as did the sublime cherry *clafoutis*. Afterwards in an intense French/English discussion we debated what to do. Carry on without the donkey? Spend the remaining time walking in the Pradelles area? Do something different altogether? But the whole point of this expedition was to walk for five days on the Stevenson Trail and to get past Cheylard l'Évêque, so that we could, as it were, put it behind us. And eventually, after consultation with Gilles, we arrived at a solution: Molly and I would carry on with the donkey – a different donkey – and Florence would simply accompany us as a walker and have nothing to do with the donkey care. As it was partly Florence's suggestion, it seemed sound. It was settled. So it was that the next day we made the acquaintance of Kenneth.

TEN GOLDEN RULES OF DONKEY MANAGEMENT

In which Molly shares the lessons learned

1. Never, ever, take a donkey's head-collar off, even at night.
2. Do not let donkey stop to eat whenever he feels like it. (Life is too short.)
3. Always carry two plastic bags. (If you rustle them, the donkey will think you've got food for him, and if it rains heavily you can put them in your boots to keep your socks dry.)
4. Always tighten the strap under his tummy ten minutes after you set off. (Otherwise you can be sure his backpack will swing round under his legs. This is not a good thing as donkeys of a nervous disposition may panic and, in any case, you're going to have to take the whole lot off and start all over again.)
5. Check regularly that his backpack is not swivelling to one side or the mat under the pack is not slipping forward, backwards, sideways, etc.
6. Never let him get his nose down if he starts pawing the ground. (It means he is about to roll on the ground and crush all your precious possessions into a *purée*.)
7. Always let him stop for a drink of clear, clean mountain water whenever the occasion presents itself. (Some donkeys don't like running water, so don't force him.)
8. Always take plenty of food and water with you at all times. (Essential for both people and donkeys.)
9. Always clean his feet and brush his coat before setting off in the mornings.
10. Whatever happens, keep calm. Don't forget you're supposed to be on holiday enjoying yourself.

GETTING READY

First catch your donkey

Easily done if you have a plastic bag and plenty of food with you and have had the foresight to leave his head-collar on.

Tie him to something

Make sure he is firmly attached to a strong, reliable structure, such as a hefty iron ring set into a stone wall, or a thick, sturdy tree trunk. (If you ignore this rule you may find he has wandered off while your back was turned: flimsy branches or trunks of saplings are no good as they may either break or bend, leaving you with the task of catching the donkey again.) The rope should be tied up short, quite high up, so he cannot get his nose down and roll. If you cannot find anything to tie him to, you'll just have to wander around after him while he snacks.

Cleaning Kenneth's hooves before setting off for the day.

Clean his feet

All that is required is a quick whizz round the inside of his feet
with that special Swiss Army Knife attachment or the special
tool that you have been given and is probably at the bottom
of the pannier. This is just to check that he hasn't anything
between his toes, so to speak (technical note: donkeys do not
have toes). If possible, do not let him lean on you, as he is a lot
heavier and stronger than you are: try jabbing him with your
elbow if he does. You're going to need all your strength for
walking up and down all those hills.

Brush him down

A quick brush to eliminate mud and leaves, etc. from the
parts where his backpack and harness will be so he will be
comfortable. Remember: this is not a beauty competition.
The donkey does not care if his mane is tangled. In fact, he
probably prefers it like that.

Put on his mat and his backpack

Care is required here. If you get it wrong to begin with you're
going to have to stop and re-organise it later, probably at the
most inconvenient time. You need the donkey-hirer to show
you how, the first time, and you should pay careful attention
to what is being done, so you can do exactly the same all by
yourself tomorrow. In fact, it is best if everyone in the group
watches and listens, particularly if you have children with you
as they are far more alert than grown-ups in the mornings and
as a general rule have far better memories.

Pack the panniers

Try and organise it so both sides weigh the same and so items
which you may need often or in a hurry (such as food, water,
sunhats, sun cream, raincoats) are easily accessible on the top.
It is discouraging to have to stop and empty the backpack to

retrieve the map which you packed at the bottom, and then again, ten minutes later, the muesli bars. Try and allow for the fact that, after lunch, the food will no longer be weighing down the backpack but your legs, so arrange the lunch equally on either side so the load is not lopsided after lunch. (There's not much to be done about your legs, unfortunately.)

Set off
This is the tricky bit as by now you usually have a crowd gathered round taking photos and jostling each other, so it is best if you've found out beforehand which way you're meant to go, otherwise you may spoil the overall impression. If ten minutes have elapsed since you tightened the strap under his tummy, tighten it again. It is very amusing for the general public if the donkey's pack swivels round under his legs before you even leave, but a trifle embarrassing for the donkey handler. If this does happen you can always ask one of the children to go round with a hat: most people will stop

Molly holding on to Kenneth while he snacks.

laughing and leave immediately or, who knows, you may even collect some money. Once you're sure you know which way to go and that the pack isn't going to fall off immediately, a pull on the nose and a push on the rump, a quick clucking noise (get the donkey-hirer to show you how to make donkey-encouraging noises) and you're away.

WALKING WITH YOUR DONKEY

The donkey handler must remain alert and ask himself or herself continuously: is my donkey following me? There are several things that can go wrong here. The donkey may have stopped in order to refresh himself with a short snack of grass, leaves or other vegetation. In this case, you must admonish him verbally and give a series of short, sharp pulls on his head-collar in order to get him to come along again. Alternatively, the donkey may have whipped past you while you were not paying attention. In this case you must not let him stay in front; you must get him behind you again. This is because a donkey in front of a person thinks he is boss in which case he will very soon pull the lead out of your hand, your arm out of its socket or stop and eat grass, or all three.

Going faster
There needs to be two of you for this: one behind slapping him on the rump and one in front pulling on the nose. A plastic bag to rustle is also a good ploy to get him going – apples, dry bread and carrots being associated in the average donkey's mind with rustling plastic bags.

Going faster still
This requires the combined efforts of three people: one person way ahead with the plastic bag, one person holding the donkey's nose and one person pushing at the rear.

Going slower

This is not usually a problem but can be difficult with lively donkeys, particularly downhill. On narrow lanes and if the donkey does not bite, walk in front of him and refuse to be rushed, even if he keeps jabbing you in the back with his nose (thick protective clothing is useful) or stepping on your heels (strong protective footwear is useful). On wide open spaces the problem is more difficult to deal with. Walking with your arms outstretched sideways is quite effective but tiring, particularly for the shoulders. Walking very fast in order to outstrip him is also tiring, particularly for the legs. Pulling him round in circles in order to keep his attention and restrict his pace is also tiring and can make you dizzy. Probably the best plan is to try a mixture of all three. Indeed, when trying to get a donkey to slow down, you realise the true meaning of the Biblical phrase 'get thee behind me, Satan'. Quite simply, it means that Jesus was used to dealing with donkeys and knew that this would be the only way to have the upper hand.

Stopping for a break

Both you and the donkey need regular food and rest breaks so find him a nice, strong tree with plenty to eat in easy reach and tie him up so he can't get his nose down (see Golden Rule no. 6). The ideal is a grassy hedgerow, where he can graze up the side of the bank, or a beech tree which usually has lots of tasty little leafy branchlets at donkey height, or, at the right time of year, brambles. Otherwise you can always share your sandwiches with him. Remember: ham is not a good choice for a donkey and he will prefer stale bread, which does not stick to his teeth. He may also like muesli bars or, more traditionally, apples, carrots, etc. Do not tie him up too far away from your picnic as donkeys are sociable creatures and you do not want him to feel left out.

STOPPING FOR THE NIGHT

This is the moment both you and the donkey have been looking forward to for hours. He needs a nice secure enclosure with lots to eat (usually the *gîte* owner will provide this), plenty of water and his head-collar on. You may find that his lackadaisical pace and look of near-exhaustion that was making you feel so guilty over the last 15km disappears miraculously once he realises you're stopping for the night. Once you've taken off the backpack and let him loose he will probably run around and roll. Most donkeys appreciate it if you go and say goodnight to them after supper but don't worry if he pretends not to recognise you: he's just getting his strength up for tomorrow.

Noisette with flowers.

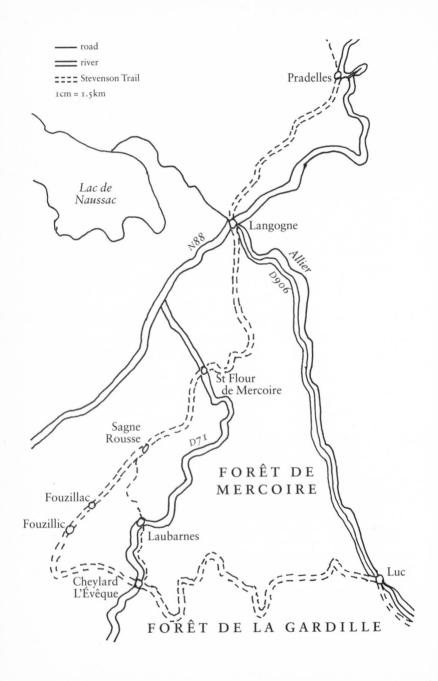

road
river
Stevenson Trail
1cm = 1.5km

Pradelles

Lac de Naussac

Langogne

N88

Allier

D906

St Flour
de Mercoire

Sagne
Rousse

D71

FORÊT DE
MERCOIRE

Fouzillac

Fouzillic

Laubarnes

Luc

Cheylard
L'Évêque

FORÊT DE LA GARDILLE

OUR FIRST MEETING WITH KENNETH
Pradelles–Luc

In which Hilary feels like a tortoise

The day Molly and I took over, Gilles' wife Suzanne took us down to the field below the village to meet Kenneth. Ten donkeys trotted immediately over to Suzanne, with her bags of stale baguettes, nuzzling and pushing us and each other. Kenneth, a sturdy three-year-old with gentle eyes was one of the most determined foragers. He was really on his day off, and was not too thrilled about having this extra engagement, it seemed. He made heavy weather of going back up the hill to the brasserie.

Once there and tethered to a nearby lamppost he appeared resigned to his fate. Gilles took Molly and me through all the rules of donkey management again – how many notches up the straps to fasten buckles, which way to clean his hoofs, which way up the panniers should go. (He was taking no chances.) Florence, dawdling inside over her coffee, was being very disciplined about her non-involvement.

And so, a year on from our first attempt, we set off south from Pradelles. The grassy path to Langogne was agreeably familiar. We ticked off the landmarks: the tree where we had rested, the ditch Whiskey had paddled in, and the blonde-maned horses (one with a foal this time). Somehow, however, we still ended up going through the centre of Langogne on market day. Kenneth was less sanguine about parked cars than Noisette had been and insisted on walking in the middle of the road. Our little procession made its way through the town at the head of a line of cars and was greeted by cheers from a pavement cafe: they turned out to be from five people who had slept in the dormitory upstairs at the *gîte*. They were on foot and untrammelled by donkey but we had overtaken them – I felt like the tortoise in Aesop's fable.

We managed to take the right route this year towards St Flour de Mercoire, so we travelled pleasantly through shady woods and alongside a delightful broad river gleaming in the sun in the bottom of the valley. Unfortunately, St Flour was not in the bottom of the valley. It was on a ridge. The next few hundred metres up and up the road in sun that had suddenly become savagely hot were gruelling. So blistering was the heat that my scalp was burning and, hatless (strangely, a hat had not been on my list), I had to wrap a tee-shirt round my head, playing the role of eccentric Englishwoman admirably. We collapsed at the horse trough on the edge of the village, ostensibly for Kenneth, who had a hearty dislike of running water, but really for us: we poured water over our heads and necks with scant regard for our appearance while Molly discoursed on plans to give up her job in Montpellier and buy a house here to run as a donkey bed-and-breakfast.

We found our way easily enough from St Flour up to Sagne Rousse. Molly and I recalled every step of this bit as though it were yesterday. After a steep climb we were into the wonderful wooded part where all was suddenly muffled, except for occasional piercing birdsong, and our feet moved softly on a spongy carpet of pine needles. We passed through the grove of gnarled trees, wondering where the cows we remembered from last year were, and found them in the field by the road, gathering to stare as we passed. This year we had time to pause in the clearings to listen first to the stillness and then to the repeated notes of a thrush, and to watch Whiskey splash ecstatically in a large puddle, pouncing on water boatmen as they glided along the surface.

As we descended into Cheylard l'Évêque – with mixed feelings about the night's lodgings – we felt more inclined than last year to appreciate the dramatic views – great fir-clad valleys plunging into ravines, a mountainside spattered yellow with broom. But at Laubarnes the black stallion in the distance did not canter over to see us as last time.

At the Refuge du Moure, Mme. Simonet remembered us from our last visit. This was not necessarily the compliment it might seem, as her memory probably stemmed from the fact that M. Simonet had thoroughly disapproved of us summoning Gilles to rescue us then from our ill-fated expedition. Perhaps our disaffection at their obsession with cleanliness had been noted. Anyway, they had found a good solution to that now: a staircase had been built on to the side of the building, so that muddy walkers could be diverted from the haven of the Simonets' home, and enter the dormitories directly through a cloakroom. Here they had to change into what a notice announced was the 'quarantine' of soft shoes 'for your comfort'. A list of rules was fixed to the wall: use the slippers, don't smoke, turn the light out, don't dry clothes on the radiators, don't steal your neighbour's new shoes. . . . Dogs, of course, were still not allowed in the house.

Anyway, it was good to have arrived. We took Kenneth to the little walled field near by where he rolled with pleasure at being free. After Molly had reluctantly settled Whiskey into the damp and distant kennel, we put our slippers on for supper.

As this was a holiday weekend, there were thirty people here – motorcyclists, car drivers, cyclists. And us, with our donkey. The only walkers. One member of a party was late for supper. He had at least realised the enormity of his misdemeanour and came in armed with a large bunch of flowers for Mme. Simonet to offset her displeasure. It didn't work. Mealtime here is sacrosanct. Understandable, perhaps, as the food is remarkable. That night the five-course meal consisted of vegetable soup, a picturesque salad of tomatoes sliced and reassembled, stuffed chicken, several unusual cheeses followed finally by rhubarb and apple tart. But, perfect though it was, we walkers felt we were there under sufferance. Muddy, wet, dirty and with too many outside clothes and animals, we sensed we were hampering the smooth running of the Refuge.

It led to acts of childish rebellion, like Molly stomping into the bedroom the next morning with her boots on. She would have brought Whiskey in with her if she thought she could have got away with it. Even Florence was mutinous. Her attempt to talk to M. Simonet about his trips to the Antarctic – his spectacular photographs hang on the walls – on the grounds that her father had been there some twenty years ago – was stiffly brushed off. Still, we reassured ourselves, we need never come here again. Our final destination on this leg of the trip was Luc, 12km away, so we could pick up the Trail from there next time.

It did cross my mind that perhaps we were being unduly harsh. Our alienation was certainly not shared by all visitors, as the guest book was full of compliments on the '*accueil chaleureux*' and the '*gastronomie grandiose*'. Le Refuge, we concluded, must attract a clean, obedient type of guest. We were obviously the wrong sort.

Today would be the first proper test of our competence, after Gilles' instruction. Molly fetched Kenneth from his haven and tied him up outside the small church. Then, while Florence dutifully feigned lack of interest, we carefully assembled the kit, threading straps, fastening buckles, scrupulously aligning the mat under the *bât* and loading the panniers. We took care and patience over each aspect.

An old man supported by two sticks hobbled over to a nearby bench to sit and watch our endeavours with keen interest. By 10:15am, with panniers perfectly packed and beautifully balanced, we led Kenneth with calm authority past his bench. We exchanged *bonjours*. '*Vous voulez nous accompagner?*' said Molly cheerfully to him, as we set off up the road. We had gone perhaps ten metres when we heard a shout from the man on the bench. We turned to see him gesticulating at Kenneth, still patiently clip-clopping along behind us. He was, however, now carrying his load slung under his tummy rather than on his back.

It struck us as remarkably funny. For a few minutes we could do nothing as we bent double in a struggle to subdue the laughter. Florence looked utterly perplexed at our merriment, but, to give her her due, she offered no help, advice or even criticism. She was keeping her end of the bargain. Eventually we managed to control ourselves, and spread all bags and belongings over the grass verge as we battled with the harness again. 'I remember now,' said Molly. 'We have to make the tummy girth much tighter, because they puff their tummy out when they are being loaded.' 'Great time to bring that up *now*,' I said sourly. And she folded up again helplessly.

After our delayed departure from Cheylard, the path was precipitous, following steep short cuts between the zigzags of a mountain road. Molly and I were doing our best with Kenneth but he must have sensed the hand of inexperience on his leading rope. As we later climbed a road winding up the side of a valley, Kenneth stopped implacably, turned his head to gaze across the valley, and then threw his head back and brayed mournfully: in the distance was a white van like the one belonging to Gilles. Our far-sighted donkey was pining for home.

By this time, Kenneth's pack was slipping again. So we spent longer than anticipated over lunch, unloading and reloading the donkey for the third time in two hours. At least we provided a diversion for an elderly couple out on a snail hunt, who watched our efforts with amusement. By the hamlet of Les Pradels our route turned off on to a flatter path, now on a level with the mountain peaks around Cheylard. We followed a lane thick with flowers – cuckooflowers and violets by the bushel – alongside a field containing a pair of bay horses. They ambled over to the fence and followed us along, their eyes fixed on Kenneth with great curiosity. Kenneth was not remotely interested, regarding them with a fine insouciance as we entered the Forêt Dominiale de la Gardille.

In the heart of the forest of dark firs, some fringed with lighter green, and all very fragrant, was Lac de Louradou – and a great convocation of people. It seemed almost shocking to us, after our isolation of the day, to see all the families, children and sunbathers (one of whom was inadvertently nearly trampled by Kenneth). They were fascinated by us. A woman holding a puppy in her arms like a baby came closer to examine our little procession, children on the jetty called and waved. Then Kenneth caught sight of the vast expanse of water, dug his hooves in and just refused to move. Our triumphant arrival was matched only by the ignominy of our departure, which took quite a long time.

Molly and Hilary repacking Kenneth's bags for the third time that day.

The last lap to the castle above Luc, dominated by its Madonna stretching her arms embracingly over the area, was downhill, narrow and between close-growing bushes, which made donkey management very difficult – unfortunate, as Kenneth liked to go very fast downhill. Because it was so strenuous, Molly and I took short turns in our attempts to restrain him. We raced past a field with a huddle of the first sheep I had seen in the Cévennes, past a tractor blaring out *Pretty Woman* on its radio, and across a junction. But at last I thought I had the measure of Kenneth. 'Who's in charge?' I cried rhetorically, as I refused to allow him to stop to eat, tapping him on his nose when he went too fast. 'I can see you are getting severe,' said Florence approvingly in a rare comment on our handling. And for a few minutes he would appear docile, until off he went again helter-skelter, dragging me in his wake.

We had for some time been longing for a beer, so we were looking forward to our rendezvous with Gilles in the bar at Luc. But the bar was closed, and we had to wait patiently and thirstily at the roadside. When he arrived, Kenneth – surprisingly, considering his apparent yearning for the white van earlier that day – was deeply reluctant to get inside. Molly was inside the van rattling a bag of donkey nuts, I was behind brandishing a switch. But I could bring myself only to feebly tap him on the rump, which had no effect all. 'Beat him, beat him,' shouted Florence, casting aside her non-interventionist policy. Despite my new-found severity, I couldn't quite bring myself to do that. Luckily Kenneth's desire for food finally did the trick.

After a mere half-hour journey Kenneth was released into his field. He looked rather pleased. Then we were released into the brasserie. *Here* was the bar we had been dreaming of. We sank down into the chairs and threw off our boots. Gilles brought us foaming beers on the house. We'd done 80km in five days. Just 140km to go.

A JOURNEY THROUGH FOOD

In which Molly cooks dishes to be found on the Trail

In order to allow you to get into the spirit of the thing and to reproduce some of the experiences of walking the Stevenson Trail in the comfort of your own home, here are a few dishes that you are likely to meet if ever you struggle out of your armchair and into your walking boots. All ingredients are for four people unless otherwise stated.

Lentils and Sausages

A typical Stevenson Trail dish, just the thing at the end of a day's walk in the rain and mountain mists. Unfortunately, indigestion is guaranteed if you eat it too late in the day.

2 tablespoons olive oil
6 *saucissons de Toulouse* (big, meaty sausages
with great chunks of meat and fat in them)
3 *oignons des Cévennes* (big, fat, fresh onions), chopped
6 garlic cloves, chopped or crushed
500g/18oz green Puy lentils, rinsed
120ml/4 fl oz red wine
120ml/4 fl oz water
salt and pepper

Put the olive oil in a big heavy-bottomed pan and fry the sausages quickly – just a little so they leak out their fat. When they've gone brown on the outside, reduce the heat and add the chopped onions. When the onions are golden, add the garlic and, immediately afterwards, pour in the lentils and cover with half red wine, half water and simmer for ages. Season to taste.

NB: Take care not to put too much salt in this dish as the sausages will spill their salt into the lentils. It's best to wait until near the end and then adjust salt level as required.

My choice of wine to go with it: a red Cahors or Costières du Gard.

Pork and Potatoes

Sometimes Gillles uses *confit de porc* (pork cooked and conserved in lots of fat in glass jars) but I think it's better fresh. A tasty dish which is rather rich but who cares once in a while? It's nice served with a green salad (or green beans), which cuts through the grease a bit, and followed by fruit or ice cream rather than a heavy pudding. This recipe requires a certain sleight-of-hand and concentration in order to synchronise meat, potatoes and sauce – even more so if you do green beans with it as well, but it's worth the stress.

1 *filet mignon* of pork
4 tablespoons olive oil
a pinch of dried or sprig of fresh thyme
a pinch of dried or sprig of fresh rosemary
1 head of garlic
8 hefty potatoes
sunflower or groundnut oil
juice of a lemon
2 tablespoons water
500ml/17 fl oz double cream

The day before, take all the bits of fat and gristle off the pork and marinade it in olive oil with thyme, rosemary and garlic (whole cloves) overnight.

On the day, preheat the oven to 150°C/300°F/gas mark 2, take the pork out of the marinade and cook it hot and quick in the olive oil in a thick-bottomed frying pan for a few minutes to seal in the juices. Then, without burning your fingers, take it out of the frying pan, cover it in tinfoil and bung it in a the pre-heated oven for two hours. Whatever you do, don't throw the fat and juice and all the little crunchy bits away out of the frying pan.

While the meat is cooking in the oven, peel the potatoes and cut them into crosswise slices as thick as chips – i.e. about 1cm/1/2in thick. Thirty minutes before you serve the meal, fry the potatoes in the sunflower or groundnut oil in another pan, turning them over regularly. You need a wide-enough frying pan to be able to do this comfortably as, if it's too small, the layer of potatoes will be too thick and the ones in the middle will go mushy. If you don't have a wide-enough frying pan, you can always make chips instead.

While the potatoes are cooking, prepare the sauce in the first pan: add the water and the lemon juice and continue to heat the mixture while you scrape all the nice tasty bits from the bottom of the frying pan. Keep cooking and stirring until it's nice and thick and then reduce the heat and add a bit of the sauce to the cream. Mix it round and then at the last minute add the cream mixture to the pan under a low heat, stir like crazy and, when it's thickened, slop it over the meat and potatoes.

The finished dish should be piping hot, very appetising, smothered and shining with sauce and grease.

My choice of wine to go with it: a rosé Cabernet d'Anjou or rosé de Provence.

Stuffed Cabbage

A traditional country dish, much prized in areas where only the cabbage can survive the rigours of winter. We had stuffed cabbage when taking the donkeys down from the their summer pasture but I think the following recipe is even nicer as there is a higher proportion of vegetables to meat. Every self-respecting *gîte* owner has their own recipe, but the following is how I like it best. In addition to a thick-bottomed pan, you will also need thin kitchen-type string to tie it up with. (You shouldn't need too much as it won't struggle in the pan: it's just to stop the leaves opening again and the stuffing falling out.)

1 nice fat crinkly cabbage
6 onions
4 garlic cloves
2 eggs
4 tablespoons breadcrumbs
6 thick bacon or pork slices, finely chopped,
or 500g/18oz minced beef
salt and pepper to taste
a handful of fresh parsley, chopped
2 carrots, sliced
50g/2oz lard
120ml/4 fl oz single cream (optional)

Blanch the cabbage in boiling water for a few minutes. Chop all the onions and the garlic apart from one onion and two garlic cloves, which you will need later. Mix the eggs, bread-crumbs, meat, chopped onion and garlic, salt and pepper to make a mushy mixture.

Take the cabbage out of the boiling water and, when it's cooled down a bit, open out its leaves like a water lily. Push the stuffing mixture down as far as possible between each leaf until you've coated the inside of each leaf and used up all the mixture. Tie the whole thing up with the string so the leaves won't open and the stuffing seep out.

Now take a large, thick-bottomed pan, deep rather than wide, preferably cast-iron, and melt the lard slowly in the bottom along with another chopped onion and the sliced carrots. Add the tied-up cabbage and a couple of garlic cloves and enough water to come half way up the side of the cabbage. Put the lid on and cook slowly, checking regularly to make sure it doesn't stick to the bottom, particularly the garlic which goes bitter and nasty if burnt. (This is why a thick-bottomed pan is necessary.) The meal is ready when the whole thing is tender, usually after an hour or an hour and a half.

Serve with plain boiled potatoes or potatoes baked in their jackets. There's no need to do anything special with the gravy which is delicious as it is, but if you want to tart it up you can mix the gravy with a little cream to thicken it.

My choice of wine to go with it: red Côtes du Rhône

Quail Salad
If you have read chapter four you will be pleased to know that this recipe features quails but without their heads. The quails we had at the Refuge du Moure *were* very tasty, but it was rather gruesome to see them staring up from the plate. Quails for the squeamish then.

First catch your quails. Alternatively you can buy them at Waitrose. In France you can get quail fillets, which are what you need for this recipe. If you can only get whole ones, just roast them plain and then take the meat off the bone and use it as explained for the fillets below except that you'll serve it as a cold rather than a hot salad.

1 large *frisée* lettuce (this sort of lettuce doesn't go floppy
when you add hot things to it, in this case hot quail fillets)
8 fresh, firm tomatoes, finely sliced

1 onion, finely sliced
1 yellow pepper, seeded and finely sliced
16 quail fillets or 8 quails (see above)
2 tablespoons raspberry vinegar (or white wine vinegar if
you can't get it)
2 tablespoons chopped fresh parsley

Pull the lettuce to bits and arrange it on a large, flat dish. Arrange the tomato and onion sparingly on the bed of lettuce (the overall colour scheme at this stage should be green with little bits of red and white). Scatter the pepper on top.

When the salad is ready and waiting, the table set and the dinner guests drooling round the table, grill the quail fillets under a hot grill (5 minutes maximum) and toss them into the salad. Sprinkle quickly with the vinegar and parsley and serve immediately. Mind, it's hot.

My choice of wine to go with it: chilled, white Jurançon sec.

L'Aligot

This is a strange, stringy mixture of potatoes and cheese, much prized by people living in the Cévennes as it is very filling and keeps out the cold. It is easy to make but requires alertness, tenacity and fairly strong arms (you have to stir it for what seems like hours). Michel at La Bastide Puylaurent made some for us, but his came out of a packet. This recipe is for the real thing.

300g/11oz Tomme d'Auvergne cheese (preferably
unmatured)
500g/18oz old potatoes (Bintje, if you can get them)
4 big sausages for grilling (optional)
100g/3 1/2oz butter
250ml/9 1/2 fl oz double cream
1 garlic clove
salt and pepper

First, find your Tomme d'Auvergne (if you can't find any locally, you will have to go to France and bring some back, as nothing else will do for this recipe). Cut it into very thin slices. If you can, leave it to stand for a day after slicing it up. (In addition to bringing out the flavour, this resting time allows you to recover from the tedium of cutting it up.)

Around an hour before you intend eating, peel and cut up the potatoes into medium pieces and boil them for 20–25 minutes, until they can be easily mashed. While they are in the pan, lay the table, open the wine and crush the garlic and put it to one side. Just before the potatoes are ready, start the sausages, if you are having them, on a slowish grill.

Drain the potatoes and mash them finely so they make a nice, smooth *purée*. Mix in the butter and cream and crushed garlic Add salt and pepper (don't overdo the salt as the cheese is salty) and return the *purée* to the pan.

Now comes the exciting bit. Put the pan on a low heat and add the thin slices of cheese and *keep stirring* in a figure of eight. Also, don't forget to keep an eye on the sausages (if they are ready before the potato and cheese mixture, keep them hot). After about 15 minutes of solid or constant stirring, the mixture in the pan will become a smooth, elastic paste which comes away cleanly from the sides of the pan. When this happens, *don't stop stirring*, call everyone, run to the table and plonk a lump of Aligot on each plate. It should refuse to separate from the spoon so you will need to cut it off using kitchen scissors. (If you find the ingredients in the pan suddenly go solid and then runny, this means your pan got too hot and you need to start all over again. Next time try reducing the heat.)

Serve it by itself or with the sizzling hot sausages.

My choice of wine to go with it: a full-bodied red such as Marcillac or Cahors.

La Poule au Pot

This is a traditional dish invented by Good King Henry (Henri IV), who wanted all his subjects to have a nice time and at least one good meal a week (see page 29). It is not restricted to the Stevenson Trail but it does give you an insight into French country cooking. Each region has its own version.

1 large, plump, middle-aged hen or boiling
fowl (not a small, skinny chicken)
The hen's liver, finely chopped (ask your butcher
to keep the liver for you when he guts the bird)
6 onions
4 cloves of garlic
500g sausage meat
a handful of chopped fresh parsley
3 or 4 egg yolks
Half a cup of breadcrumbs
4 sticks of celery
6 carrots
6 leeks
4 fresh tomatoes or a small tin of peeled tomatoes
500ml/18 fl oz water
6 potatoes, peeled
salt and pepper

First, make the stuffing by chopping up two of the onions and the garlic and add them to the sausage meat and chopped liver, along with the chopped parsley. Mix thoroughly and add two egg yolks and then the breadcrumbs and a little salt and pepper to make a moist mixture. You may need to add a third egg yolk in order to make it moist enough.

Make sure there are no other organs left lurking in the hen and then fill the cavity with the stuffing and sew the hen back up again.

Take the remaining vegetables except the potatoes, chop them roughly and bring them to the boil in a large pan with half a litre or so of water. Drop the hen in and simmer it for an hour and a half to two hours. You may need to add more water, so check it from time to time. The juice should be a nice orangey colour. Half an hour before the end of cooking, add the potatoes.

You can serve it with its own juice, or you can make a *sauce poulette* i.e. a white sauce to which you have added some of the juice from the pan along with another egg yolk. Be careful when you do this that the mixture isn't too hot or it will curdle.

Adjust seasoning to taste and serve piping hot on a large dish with the hen in the middle (which hopefully some kind soul will chop into quarters for you) and the vegetables around it, with the sauce on top or in a sauce dish.

My choice of wine to go with it: a white Anjou or Val de Loire. King Henry's favourite wine, however, was a Givry (or so says the signpost leading into the village of Givry, near Beaune).

Acacia tree.

Beignets d'Acacia

This is a dish to be found in May in the southernmost part of the Trail only (where the acacia tree grows). It uses the delicate, perfumed white flowers of *Robinia pseudoacacia* to produce an unusual and delicious dessert. Be particularly careful in your choice of flowers, which should be gathered from a spot where there is no pollution, otherwise you'll have to wash them and you'll wash away the flavour as well. Also be careful not to confuse acacia flowers (which are white and edible) with laburnum flowers (which are yellow and very poisonous). If you grow your own courgettes, you can try this recipe with courgette flowers.

2 eggs
3 egg whites
250ml/9 fl oz of beer
sunflower oil
salt
250g/9oz of flour
12 sprigs of acacia flowers with tender stems
20g/1oz of sugar
oil for deep frying

Beat the eggs and egg whites in a bowl. Add the beer, a drop or two of sunflower oil and a pinch of salt. Stir the flour in gradually until you have a nice, smooth mixture.

Heat the oil in a deep frying pan. Dip the flower sprigs into the batter so as to coat them. Then deep fry them for a few minutes, turning them when they go brown. As soon as they are brown on both sides, take them out and drain them on kitchen paper. Sprinkle with sugar and serve immediately.

My choice of wine to go with it: a Sauternes (or a nice cup of tea).

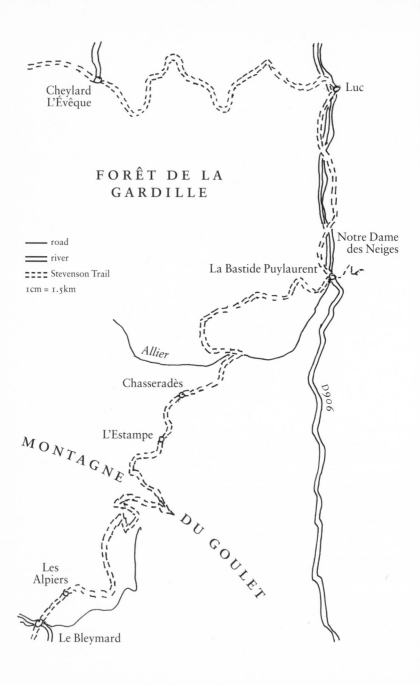

Cheyland
L'Évêque

Luc

FORÊT DE LA
GARDILLE

——— road
═══ river
▪▪▪▪ Stevenson Trail
1cm = 1.5km

Notre Dame
des Neiges

La Bastide Puylaurent

Allier

Chasseradès

L'Estampe

D906

MONTAGNE

DU GOULET

Les
Alpiers

Le Bleymard

AUTUMN IN THE CÉVENNES
Luc–Le Bleymard

In which Hilary takes a ride with Kenneth

We returned to the Cévennes the following autumn. It was surprisingly easy to entice Kenneth away from the other donkeys and into the van, that September day. The bucket of oats probably helped. But we liked to think that it was also because he recognised us. Of the three donkeys we had hired, Kenneth was by far and away our favourite. Noisette had rivalled Stevenson's uncooperative Modestine and walked even more slowly than I did. Jeep didn't like dogs, which was problematic. Kenneth, on the other hand, soft-coated and dark-eared, had a pragmatic and accommodating nature. His only flaw was a tendency to race downhill.

Just before we arrived at the Brasserie du Musée the day before, Molly had fleetingly wondered whether she should have rung to remind Gilles that we were coming. She had contacted him to say that we, plus two friends, wanted to do the next stage, but that had been a while before. This time our companions were two friends of Molly: Véro and Dany. Véro, who worked in a pharmacy, was volatile and fast-talking; Dany, a jewellery saleswoman, had had a jet-set former life and was elegant and calm.

Gilles did indeed look surprised to see us. We wanted a donkey when? '*Demain*,' said Molly. He looked thoughtful. He had the donkeys, *bien sûr*, but the van to transport the donkey to the beginning of the next section was in the garage. He began to make phone calls. We weren't worried; we knew he would sort it out.

We went to the *gîte d'étape*, rearranged all our belongings in bin liners and bags, and took Whiskey for a walk. Below the mountain-top village – 1100 metres up – there was a blanket of thick heavy cloud, but up here the sun was setting, a wild September sunset, tingeing lighter, whiter clouds with pink and gold. It seemed a good omen. This time we had come in the month when RLS had set out on his travels. Instead of mountains spread with spring flowers, the verges and hedgerows were full of fruit – wild strawberries, late raspberries, blackberries: handy if we got lost again, at least.

This stage, from Luc to Mont Lozère, would be strictly French-speaking, Molly had warned: Véro and Dany spoke no English. Over supper the first night (salad and paté, ham, *confit de porc* and potatoes, plus a variety of local cheeses and fruit), I could catch about one word in three. My talking was better: as I laboriously described a weekend in Paris to Gilles, Véro broke in, speaking at breakneck speed, and Molly translated: 'She's very impressed with your grasp of the past subjunctive.'

Gilles did indeed sort things out on the transport front. He retrieved his van from the garage the next morning and we drove in convoy, Gilles transporting Kenneth, Véro and me in the van, Molly and Dany in their cars, to the ruined Château de Luc, the only 'notable feature' in Luc, according to RLS, with its '50 quintals of brand-new Madonna' on the tower. Kenneth was moored to a tree while Gilles patiently explained, yet again, the rules of donkey handling. Then Molly and Dany drove the cars to the next port of call, with Gilles following on in his van to bring Molly and Dany back to Luc. Meanwhile, Whiskey raced round madly in circles as a nearby donkey bellowed conversationally at Kenneth.

Finally we set off on our travels, the not-so-new Madonna's hands raised in benediction over our little procession. Down in the town, Dany and I visited the church –

very simple, with a wooden balcony and smelling of old damp stone – and lit candles: no harm in hedging our bets with a little divine guidance. Within minutes of leaving the church, we had taken the wrong turning. So much for divine guidance.

We retraced our steps to a pleasant stream: time for lunch already, we thought. This was the pattern of our journey: we would overcome some minor vicissitude and felt this major achievement merited a food break. We made sure that we were provided with food enough for many such breaks.

Finally on the right path, we pushed on up the path towards the hamlet of La Fraisse, where we met two walkers on their own food break, sitting on the verge with their

Castle at Luc, with its statue of the Madonna.

shoes off. They gallantly got to their feet to greet us – they seemed almost to be expecting us. It turned out that when they had stayed in Pradelles Gilles had told them that they might meet an English lady with a donkey. They were taking nine days to do the whole Trail, which seemed horribly impressive to us – but then they did not have a donkey to assist them.

Our real destination was the Trappist monastery of Notre Dame des Neiges, site of much philosophising and religious disputation by RLS. Despite the hospitality offered to Modestine, the monastery is not on the official Stevenson Trail so we stayed instead in La Bastide Puylaurent. Kenneth was billeted in a pleasant white-fenced meadow with white horses, while we were in the cream-coloured hotel with violet shutters opposite the station. The owner of Hotel Le Gévaudan, Michel, was intending to do some work to make this a recognised donkey stop but, as he lay on a great leather sofa much of the time watching television, that seemed an unlikely goal.

But he had apple trees and chickens, which meant platters of apples everywhere and fresh-laid, deliciously eggy boiled eggs for our breakfast. So fresh that, he told us as he served us, he had been pecked by one hen because he had tried to take the egg before she'd quite finished laying it. A little indelicate, Molly said.

On our day trip to Notre Dame, buffeted by wind, Kenneth was being unduly headstrong and it required a four-person operation to manoeuvre him – one before, one behind and one each side of his head: 'Modestine!' a villager chuckled in recognition. It took about an hour and a half to reach Notre Dame along a pleasant slowly rising path and past a herd of brown cows that had Dany in raptures. We all had to stop to watch them chomping on grass, curling their tongues round a bunch of grass and tugging at it. They were, it is true, very pretty – a soft buttery-brown with black-smudged eyes which looked as if their eyeliner had run.

As we finally arrived at Notre Dame, the clock was striking twelve. Just in time for Sexte, one of the religious offices punctuating the monks' day. We tied Kenneth to a tree and followed two women scurrying from the *maison de retraite* into the church. For the next fifteen minutes we were immersed in a world that moved at an even slower pace than we were accustomed to on the Trail. Rows of white-robed monks faced each other, singing psalms as had been done for centuries. As the service ended, five monks left and the rest were cast into attitudes of contemplation, immobile for several minutes. Dany and I stood at the back and for a few minutes it was possible for us too to experience that calm, that steady concentration of prayer, until three tolls of the bell released them.

And us too. We adjourned to the large monastery shop, which stocked all manner of honey, wine and liqueurs, nougat and even custard powder of different flavours, which is how the monastery makes its living, and filled Kenneth's panniers. There was a long bar running along the wall, where we were served little white cups of hot chocolate so thick that the spoon almost stood up in it. The chatty young man behind the counter then offered us liqueur, a little like Chartreuse. That warmed us up.

Later, back in La Bastide, when we had dismantled the donkey, we went shopping again, this time at the village shop. This was a very good shop, which – as we discovered – sold everything from all sizes of exercise books (I bought ten) to hats (I bought one of them too) to books (and a book), shoes and baby clothes. At the baker we bought bilberry tarts and took them back to the hotel, and ate them with our coffee at the bar. It was one of the advantages of Michel being so relaxed (our bedroom keys, left on the counter that morning, were still sitting there).

That evening, however, Michel roused himself to make *raclette*, a dish special to mountainous parts of France. This involves an elaborate method of melting cheese, in electric frying pans plugged into table sockets, which is then poured over whatever vegetables and *charcuterie* are to hand. It was accompanied by cold red wine in beer bottles. Maybe Michel was suffering from loneliness. He livened up after supper, playing music and even jigging on his own in front of the fragrant wood fire, its three great logs crumbling into molten ash.

The next day dawned loudly – Michel, full of energy for once (he was closing up for two days to go to the city) was

Kenneth and Michel outside his hotel at La Bastide Puylaurent.

playing a brass band reveille – and mistily. A cloud appeared to be sitting in the station car park. We climbed into the pine forest and deeper into the cloud. We could barely see more than a few metres in front of us. We had to make do with the minutiae of life on the verge: spider's webs, for example, festooned among the broom, each thread strung with beads of moisture. We watched a spider – golden with a pearly sheen and a shield-like design on its back – until Whiskey, curious at our focussed attention, blundered in, breaking the web and carrying the spider on his coat until we restored it to home turf to start the rebuild.

We lunched at a picnic table, huddled in hats and scarves, but as we descended the fog lifted, and we could see valleys, mountains and hedges heavy with blackberries. We, and Kenneth, gorged ourselves. And so we arrived at the Hôtel des Sources at Chasseradès on a glorious sunlit evening in great good humour. Kenneth was quartered in a grassy enclosure under bright-berried rowan trees and we in interconnecting rooms with antique wooden beds.

Our meal that evening was significant for being posh – it was served by a white-jacketed waiter – and elaborate: soup, salad, paté, *blanquette de veau*, cheese and a redcurrant pudding. At last Dany had come into her own. Each night she had sought to keep up standards by changing for dinner into sequinned tops and velvet trousers. She never let herself go, wearing make-up every day. Even the dank fog had not deterred Dany from stopping in mid-path to get out her pocket mirror and adjust her lipstick, which had rather amazed Molly and me.

Breakfast was not in the dining room but in the little room at the front of the hotel. There were three other sets of guests: a retired couple (a woman who smiled a lot and a man who didn't), a middle-aged couple with a rather plump boy (why was he not in school, we wondered) and a man whom we had already met at La Bastide. He had come from the station to the hotel just as Michel was closing up. He had managed to arrive in Chasseradès before us (not so many food stops probably). Here, he spent most of breakfast time talking – but not apparently to anyone. On our way out of town, we saw him outside the village hotel with a glass of red wine. It was 10am. 'Ah,' exclaimed Molly with an air of enlightenment, 'that explains it.'

Loading up the donkey under the rowan trees had been a pleasant experience, especially for me, watching from the other side of the road. But I had done my bit – and while cleaning Kenneth's hooves, I had been kicked on my hand for my efforts. Molly gave me tiny arnica tablets to place under my tongue. 'It will prevent bruising,' she said confidently. I wasn't entirely convinced.

Our magisterial cavalcade made its way past staring bystanders and a St Bernard – yesterday loudly aggressive, today dropping his jaw in respectful astonishment at the sight of the donkey – past cemetery and church, and out of Chasseradès. When RLS was in Chasseradès, the 'company in the inn . . . were all men employed in survey for one of the projected railways'. We could see the fruits of their labours – the great viaduct of Mirandol stalking across the valley. That was what we were aiming for. We followed the pretty path downwards to the floor of the valley, stopping to gaze up at the gigantic arches framing a deeply blue sky and at the swifts darting in and out, then climbed steeply up to the level of the railway, where we paused again to watch a train making its cautious way across the viaduct.

There was so much to look at: rosehips in hedges, fields of autumn crocus and trees turning gold and red. We pointed them out to each other, full of the joys of September. In a field on the edge of the hamlet of L'Estampe we stopped for lunch, pleased with our progress and the demeanour of the donkey, and then looked at the map. We had taken two hours to do two kilometres.

The rest of the day was a bit of a blur as we sought to make up lost time through the Goulet forest and past the tumbled remains of the deserted village of Serremejan on a grassy lane. Once, as we stopped on a secluded forest path to reassemble the donkey's *bât* (which had slipped because we'd forgotten, again, to tighten his girth), we met two more walkers. They looked fresh and bright. Not only was this because they did not have a donkey, but, I belatedly realised, no rucksacks either. At the hotel, we saw their bags, labelled Sherpa Expeditions. This was, in Molly's view, cheating.

After we found the source of the River Lot (where Véro valiantly crawled under a fence to the water's edge to fill the dog's bowl for Kenneth) the going got easier as we followed it downhill, except for a brief runaway by Kenneth, upset by a cyclist clad in lurid Lycra. The last few kilometres were along a charming leafy narrow lane (late raspberries lurking in the hedgerow) with a sign severely admonishing passers-by not to pick mushrooms without a permit. This did not deter Véro, who had been industriously collecting mushrooms all day.

In spite of our afternoon anxieties, it was not even dusk as we made our way through what was almost our last port of call, Les Alpiers – old crooked buildings with onions drying on the low walls and satellite dishes fastened to high ones – where we met another walker: a teacher of English. He was very impressed by the quality of Véro's and Dany's French, convinced as he was that we must all be British because we were on the Stevenson Trail.

It was still light when we arrived in Le Bleymard and disposed of Kenneth in a field behind the hotel with a wheelbarrow full of horse nuts. Véro gave the hotelier the bag of mushrooms she had collected (which, rather to our relief, were deemed not to be '*comestible*'), drank celebratory beers at the pavement tables and ate chestnut-crammed Salade Stevenson – what else? – for supper.

The next day, 22 September, was the day Stevenson began his travels with a donkey and the day we abandoned ours. We were delighted to discover when we woke up that the weather was abysmal: the rain was falling in torrents. We summoned Gilles and togged ourselves in our waterproofs to amble round Le Bleymard and gather damsons, by invitation from their owner, from a heavily laden tree.

I did wonder how Gilles was going to transport us all back to base. But he always had a solution. After installing Kenneth in the van, Gilles picked up two folding chairs from the corner and snapped them open with a flick of the wrist. So Dany and I travelled back in style alongside Kenneth, Dany managing, as usual, to look entirely elegant as she sat with her legs crossed, telling me of her trips to exotic places.

Though the rain had stopped by now, we didn't regret our change of plan. RLS might well have scorned our lack of resolve, but Mont Lozère could wait for another year.

Old house in Le Bleymard.

A JOURNEY THROUGH
FLORA AND FAUNA

In which Molly tells unscientifically of plants and insects

Happily, Stevenson chose an itinerary which, although it has several very steep bits, includes all sorts of different terrain that has remained completely unspoilt. It is a joy to walk along country lanes on wooded hillsides, discovering fantastic views and an ever-changing variety of feasts for the eye and, sometimes, for the stomach.

The first bit from Le Monastier down to Langogne (the Margeride) is an ancient granite-based plateau interspersed with volcanic and marshy areas with black soil and exaggeratedly green grass. Deep, steep-sided valleys (containing the village of Goudet and the source of the River Loire, for example) cut across it at intervals for the special purpose of reinforcing your leg muscles ready for the next 200km. If you are walking on this part in rainy weather you can easily get bogged down in the lanes with a vile-smelling mixture of mud and cowpats seeping into your boots. The edges of streams also tend to be unsuitable for sitting next to for the same reason. However, in spring these fields are a delight for the eye, being full of an incredible variety of wildflowers such as cowslips, violets, orchids, buttercups, milkmaids, cow parsley, pheasant eye narcissi, lilac and broom, all out at once. Occasionally you may see such rare plants as gentians or arnica plants flowering in the open meadows or on the edges of the footpath.

In the fields that do not feature lush pasture, rampant wildflowers and cows, you will often see small insignificant-looking lentil plants. The soil here is so rich that the lentils have their own particular flavour and have thus been awarded their own *appellation d'origine contrôlée*, just like wine.

Just after Langogne, you come to the edge of the massive, ancient forest called the Forêt de Mercoire. Originally made up of beech, silver birch and fir, it now alternates replanted forestry pines with open moorland sporting broom and bracken. Here, the boggy edges of streams are home for rare plants such as bogbean, the very pretty yellow marsh cinquefoil and the carnivorous sundew used in homeopathic medicine. Although the golden swathes of broom are very pretty, they are also an indication of the massive depopulation of the area as they colonise previously farmed ground. When RLS was blazing his Trail, the population in the countryside, and the land use, was far greater than it is today.

The Forêt de Mercoire is also the rising point for several rivers and streams including the River Lot (which later meanders over to the Garonne to provide pretty countryside for holiday homes). In the hedgerows, if you take the time to stop and stare, you may see praying mantises, grasshoppers and many sorts of butterfly, including the rare brimstone butterfly and black-veined white butterfly. Actually you do not need to stop and stare to see butterflies, as they are flitting about everywhere on sunny summer days. In the summer and autumn you can pick wild raspberries, strawberries, bilberries (or blueberries or whinberries, depending on where you come from) and blackberries.

The other things to pick and eat as you go along are the many varieties of wild mushroom so beloved of the French, who can

Arnica plant.

be seen bent-backed, scouring the forest floor from September onwards. But beware: it is best to have any mushrooms you pick checked out, as some are deadly and some of the most lethal ones look similar to some of the most prized ones. An informed opinion is needed. Any self-respecting French pharmacy has a mushroom expert who will be able to advise you, but unfortunately there are not too many pharmacies along the Trail. Depending on where you find your mushrooms you may have to carry them with you for several days, in which case they will have gone bad or be full of maggots and therefore inedible, so really it is best to take an expert with you, or forget the whole thing. The other inconvenient thing about mushrooms is that they need cooking, unlike the rest of the edible delights of the Trail, which can be nibbled as you are walking, adding an extra dimension of pleasure.

Something you should definitely not eat when walking the Trail is any part of the laburnum or mountain ash, which thrive in large areas of the route. All of the parts (flowers, leaves and berries) are highly poisonous and should be admired from a distance.

After the Forêt de Mercoire comes the uphill stretch of Mont Lozère, the top of which is so high and bleak it is above the tree line. Here, open moor and grassland with incredible views provide grazing for sheep but little sustenance for anyone else. Medicinal mountain plants, such as pussy toes (*Antennaria dioica*), which is good for sore throats and coughs, grow here – all the more medicinal for having struggled to survive in the harsh environment. Surprisingly, the French word for this plant, *pied-de-chat*, is very close to the English name. I expect it is a word that is not used much and so has not had the chance to evolve. Personally, I have only used it three times in my whole life. (Normally the French equivalents of English expressions are quite different, such as '*filer à l'anglaise*' meaning 'to take French leave'.)

The vegetation on Mont Lozère is organised according to altitude, almost as if the designer had been consulting a textbook. Highest are the pines and firs, then beech trees and, below them, the sweet chestnut trees so important for Cévennes dwellers. Chestnut wood, traditionally used for beams, doors, shutters and coffins, is naturally insect- and rot-resistant. All ancient buildings here are stone-built with their lintels made of chestnut. It is still used today in the building industry as a high-quality, ecologically sound alternative to despoiling tropical rain forests for exotic wood. Despite this, France has the unenviable world record for the importation of uncertified exotic wood (along with the highest number of nuclear power stations per square

L'arbre à pain: the chestnut tree.

metre). The edible part of the chestnut tree is, of course, the chestnut, which used to provide locals with their staple diet of chestnut flour (they used to call the chestnut tree *l'arbre à pain* or 'the bread tree') before they all moved into the towns and started eating baguettes.

South of Mont Lozère the hills and valleys get even steeper and are covered in loose shale, traditionally used as a roofing material. Right at the southern tip of the Trail, you cross from acid soil with chestnut trees to chalky terrain, uneven and stony underfoot, with small, scrubby, spiky juniper bushes, evergreen oaks and fig trees – an area known as the *garrigue*. The edible delights in this part of the Trail mainly consist of blackberries and lush, juicy, delicious figs – if you can get at them at the right time. This is not as easy as it sounds because, although wild fig trees produce two sets of fruit per year, only one set is edible. This is because they have devised a complicated symbiotic arrangement for the comfort of the fig wasp, which fertilises their flowers. The first set of fruit is produced only for the homemaking purposes of the wasp in question and is totally inedible. One of their two sets of blossom per year also looks like a fruit but isn't, so one way or another, your chances of coming across real, edible figs are slim. In the unlikely event of coming across a fig tree with edible, ripe fruit which is accessible (fig trees quite often grow out of sheer rock faces overlooking chasms), you should be careful of wasps (real wasps, not fig wasps) hiding in the middle. It is not uncommon for inattentive people to get stung in the mouth after chomping on feeding wasps. On the whole, though, there are fewer wasps (real ones) to be found on the Stevenson Trail than on an average English picnic.

The *garrigue* is the result of one of the earliest ecological blunders. It is all the fault of prehistoric man, who overgrazed his sheep and goats on the original forest, thereby destroying the vegetation, in turn causing erosion of the topsoil, which is now very thin and poor. Only very tough, evergreen plants needing little water can thrive. Prehistoric man seems to have been rather busy as he did the same thing all around the Mediterranean with the same results. In Corsica and Malta where the soil is acid, the result low-profile dense shrubland is called the *maquis*, whereas here the soil is chalky with drought-resistant, chalk-tolerant plants such as holm or evergreen oaks, turpentine pistacia or terebinth, juniper, Mediterranean buckthorn, prickly ivy, rosemary, thyme and lavender.

However, despite the disadvantages of thin, poor topsoil, in early April the *garrigue* manages to produce some exquisite miniature flowers, including deep golden daffodils only 10cm high and tiny, highly perfumed lemon- or violet-coloured irises, as fragile as tissue paper, which I first mistook for small plastic bags, there were so many of them scattered about. Later, many different sorts of small orchid appear, some of which are quite decorative but many have strange-looking shapes in dingy brown colours. In May, the *garrigue* perks up again when the cistus bushes produce masses of pink or purple flowers. These each last only one day but as there are so many it doesn't matter. However, as soon as summer comes and it gets really hot all the flowers wither and drop off and the *garrigue* goes back to being relentlessly grey-green and spiky. The only exceptions I have seen are some really beautiful blue star-like flowers (*Aphyllanthes monspeliensis*) which collapse as soon as you pick them (you are allowed to pick wildflowers in France as long as you're not in a National Park). Anyway, you do not want to be walking the Stevenson Trail in summer, it is far too hot. You'd be better off basking by someone's swimming pool, sipping cool drinks, or exploring the fjords of Norway.

But if you are walking the Trail in May, south of St Germain de Calberte you will find blossoming acacia trees growing on the banks of streams (remember the acacia *beignets*) and pretty, pale yellow mullein growing along the roadside. These plants are obviously still there if you walk the Trail at some other time of the year, but not in flower.

On the whole I cannot help feeling that Stevenson chose his path with a great deal of taste and foresight from the flora and fauna point of view. Just suppose he had chosen to walk from Lyon to Avignon: today we would have to struggle along the side of the A7 motorway, asphyxiated by petrol fumes and grateful to see a dandelion. But as it is, he has provided us with an excellent excuse for spending days and days wandering around in the depths of beautiful, unspoilt countryside, admiring flowers and birds and insects. Thank you, RLS.

Garrigue, featuring rocks and spiky bushes, between St Étienne Vallée Française and St Jean du Gard.

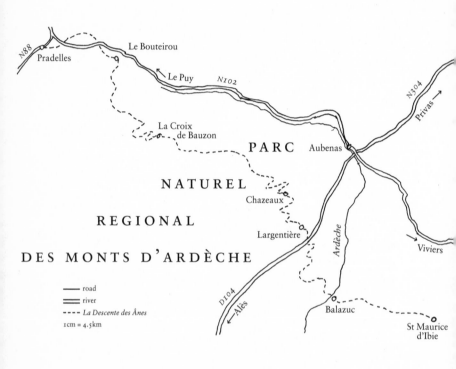

N88

Pradelles

Le Bouteirou

Le Puy

N102

La Croix
de Bauzon

PARC

Aubenas

N304

Privas

NATUREL

Chazeaux

REGIONAL

Largentière

Ardèche

DES MONTS D'ARDÈCHE

Viviers

——— road
══ river
- - - - La Descente des Ânes
1cm = 4.5km

D104

Alès

Balazuc

St Maurice
d'Ibie

LA DESCENTE DES ÂNES
Pradelles–St Maurice d'Ibie

In which Molly goes without lunch

It was October and time for the donkeys to be taken down to their winter pasture. This year Gilles wanted to try walking them down instead of taking them in the van as he usually did. He'd mentioned the idea to Hilary, Florence and me over one of his excellent foaming glasses of beer at the end of our last trip. It had sounded idyllic. There would be eight of us humans and a total of thirteen donkeys to walk peacefully from Pradelles in the Haute Loire to St Maurice d'Ibie in the Ardèche (around 100km) over a period of five days. Florence and I jumped at the chance; Hilary couldn't make it because of a long-planned trip to China.

When Florence and I arrived, after a pleasant and remarkably cheap train ride from Nîmes to Langogne, we found Gilles in his usual state of stress and excitement. He had sorted out a route that would avoid roads as much as possible. He had already tested most of the route the previous week when he had organised a similar trip taking the dozen or so horses from his riding stable down to their winter pastures near by. The only difference was that the previous week they had ridden the horses and so had been able to cover more ground per day than we could. We would be walking along with the donkeys just as if we were going along the Stevenson Trail. However, the big bonus was that the luggage would not have to be loaded on the donkeys' backs but taken by van to each night's lodging. What foresight and organisation! We were impressed.

We had a large, convivial meal that night at the Brasserie du Musée and got to know some of our fellow walkers: Suzanne,

Gilles' wife; Robert, Gilles brother; and Valérie, who helped in the bar and in the riding stables. The other two people in our party, Odette and Jacques – long-time friends of Gilles and Suzanne – were due to arrive the following morning.

Florence and I staggered off to the *gîte* after supper with strict instructions to be prompt at the bar for breakfast for an early start the following morning. After a record-breaking rapid breakfast we found Gilles had been very busy and had cunningly assembled all the donkeys together in a small field at the back of the bar. This was, in fact, the first time they had all met each other because usually they were scattered in several fields, and often one or another of them would be somewhere along the Stevenson Trail. He wanted them to get acquainted with each other and sort out who was boss before we set off, in order to avoid trouble when we were walking. He was slightly disturbed to find there were only twelve donkeys and not thirteen as he had previously calculated. However, once he and Suzanne had mulled this over, counted them several times and finally concluded that no donkeys were in fact missing, his organisational skills rapidly reasserted themselves and he assigned us to our donkeys for the next five days, as follows:

- Suzanne had two donkeys: Lola and Loustic (which means 'big and boisterous' in Languedoc).
- Florence had two donkeys: Eugénie and her daughter Manon (Eugénie had only one eye but was very maternal: she had two offspring, Manon and Loustic, and had acted as foster mother of Lola. She also had a mean streak and nipped Florence when her back was turned).
- Valérie had one and a half donkeys: Muscade and three-month-old baby Nino (he was very sweet, all long legs and thick, cuddly fur).
- Odette had one donkey, who was nameless (we later named him Lutin, or 'forest elf').

- Robert had two donkeys: Lulu and another nameless donkey (later named Larron, or 'naughty boy').
- Gilles had two donkeys: Jeep and Karamel
- Jacques had the van (a real van, not a donkey named 'Van').
- I was assigned two old friends: Kenneth the donkey and my dog Whiskey.

Just in case you're wondering why so many of the donkeys have names beginning with L, I should explain that animals in France are like cars used to be in the UK: they are assigned a letter according to the year they were manufactured, and Gilles had bought or bred most of his donkeys two years previously. Alert readers will have already worked out that Jeep was a year older than Kenneth, and Eugénie was very old indeed. (Perhaps Noisette wasn't named according to this system or perhaps she was twenty-three years old when we first met her – quite possible as donkeys do live a long time.)

Day one was fine. We set off, the sun shone and shortly afterwards we stopped for lunch and had a party with pastis, *saucisson*, roast pork, red wine, various cheeses, fruit, coffee, as well as Armagnac for us and a bottle of milk for baby Nino. Fully restored, we set off again. The grass was springy under our feet. The sky was blue. The path was well marked

with little donkey emblems on the trees. We laughed and chatted as we went along, through pine forests where lichen gatherers were loading armfuls of lichen-covered twigs into the boots of their cars. They sell these

Water pump in Pradelles.

twigs to perfume manufacturers in Grasse as lichen is a fixing agent for perfume. In the spring, the same people gather violets for the same firms. The hours are long, the work is tedious and the money is not good but it all helps make ends meet in this lonely part of France where the only thriving industry is the tourist industry – and, after all, they were out and about in some of the most beautiful country in the world.

The *gîte* for the night was comfortable, the food was good (*chou farci*), the view was marvellous, the people were friendly, the fireplace was enormous. Only Whiskey was disappointed because the *gîte* had another male dog and first we spoilt his fight and then we shut him in the van for the night.

Day two started in thick mist, in which no donkeys were to be seen. However, a quick yodel from Gilles and they came running up the hill. By the time we'd fed them and loaded them up, the mist had lifted and the sun was shining. Again we walked up through lovely pinewoods along enchanting woodland paths which led through golden autumn colours.

Trailing across mountain-tops, between Le Bouteirou and La Croix de Bauzon.

A long time (four hours) and a long way (12km) afterwards we stopped for lunch, but not before Whiskey had been stood on by Kenneth. However, his limp wore off quite quickly and we finally climbed up to the picnic place at Le Col du Pendu (Hangman's Hill) in perfect harmony. We tied the donkeys to the numerous beech trees carefully clustered for the purpose, we flung ourselves down on the thick, crackly, warm carpet of leaves and had another party (pastis, red wine, coffee, Armagnac and *saucisson*, the last of the roast pork and some cheese). Gilles went round with a gigantic syringe and huge tube tossed over one shoulder, squirting down the throat of each donkey its winter dose of thick, white worm powder. (It wasn't powder, though, it was more like sludge.)

At this point we had already climbed to 1430m but after lunch we went on climbing. By now the laughing and chattering had stopped. The beech woods were left behind us. We walked in silence on springy grass and heather and thought deep thoughts or thought no thoughts at all. There is a state of waking – a walking coma or suspended animation – which comes to the donkey walker after long distances and large meals. It is, I believe, close to the state striven for by people who practise meditation or who spend long hours watching tropical fish in an aquarium. You can feel your brain unwrinkle and your forehead too. The world slides slowly past without troubling you. The momentous decisions and cares of yesterday fade into insignificance. As a result I can't remember any more about that day except that we stopped that night in a deserted ski station (deserted because it was the wrong time of year for skiers).

On day three, we had a change in our ranks. Jacques' hip had given up somewhere among the beech woods so he was replaced by his brother Jean-Louis, who runs a local radio station. As befits an ex-disc jockey, Jean-Louis talked a lot. He was full of bounce and enthusiasm, which contrasted strongly with the rest of us, except Gilles. By this time, Gilles had taken over the van driving and had devised a complicated system enabling him to do the day's walk and drive the van. This involved driving ahead in the van (with his motorbike inside) to the night's *gîte*, leaving the bike there, driving the van back to the starting point, doing the day's walk with us, then, on arrival at the *gîte*, driving the bike back to the day's starting point, putting the bike in the back of the van and driving the van with motorbike over to the *gîte*. Then doing the same thing all over again the following day.

Day three was scheduled to be gruelling but spectacular (25km along mountain ridges with astounding views). It turned out to be merely gruelling (27km in thick mist). We climbed (yes, still climbing) through thick forest where they were shooting wild boar. (A large sign was propped across the path as we left the ski resort: 'Danger of death. Wild boar shoot in progress. Proceed at your own risk.') We didn't hear or see any more of the hunters but we learnt from Robert that the wild boar in this particular part of France are inedible because of a campaign to eradicate moles on the mountain-tops which has resulted in the entire food chain being poisoned. Hunters who bag wild boar now have to have them analysed for strychnine before settling down to their jolly hunter's feast and for several years have had to throw away all the boar they shoot.

There was a cold wind on the mountain ridge, which did not disperse the mist but simply blew it around and excited the donkeys. We had a slipping donkey pack, shortly followed by a runaway. Lulu got the wind up his tail and devised a new game of loitering innocently until everyone had gone past him and then sneaking up from the rear to attack donkey or dog, as the fancy took him. All this excitement took us up to lunchtime, but at the pre-selected spot the wind was howling so hard that we pushed on over the ridge and down into a fairly sheltered hollow. This was to be our last lavish lunch. We finished the pastis, the *saucisson*, and started the *grattons* (made from all the tiny bits left in the roasting pan, squeezed of excess grease and pressed into a sort of paté) that Jean-Louis had brought.

In the course of the afternoon even Jean-Louis fell silent as we descended from the open mountainside through beech forests with rolling pebbles underfoot and then into mixed chestnut and pine woods. Donkeys like chestnuts so we gave them handfuls to encourage them onwards. 'Only 300 metres to go,' announced Gilles as we slid from the path on to a tiny steep road dropping into the valley. The valley was wonderful. It had palm trees and fig trees and vines and tiny overgrown fields and little ruined houses and tiny streams. An ancient little old man came out of his cottage and presented Kenneth with an apple. It felt like coming into a different world. Rather like I imagine Hannibal and his troops felt when they came down out of the Alps and found themselves in Italy.

Half an hour later, we were still walking down magical narrow paths, under abandoned apple trees, alongside enchanting streams, and we still hadn't got to our destination. Then, rounding a last corner: 'There,' said Gilles, 'there's our stable'. The stable was for us; the donkeys had to sleep in a field. Unlike the other places we had stayed, there was no food laid on. There were not even any beds and the mattresses arranged under the eaves were stained and not very appealing. We set loose the donkeys, plodded to the stable, sat down and took our shoes off. It was better to be sitting down but even without moving we could see there was a severe shortage of creature comforts, which dampened our spirits rather. After a rest, things improved. We borrowed two large pans from the owner of the stables in which to cook spaghetti carbonara, and Jean-Louis rang his wife on his mobile and asked her to bring some more wine. Some of us had hot showers in the makeshift toilet area. I didn't. I didn't fancy paddling through the dirty water on the floor to get to the shower. That night I slept in my clothes in my padded sleeping bag on my macintosh, determinedly dirty but well insulated from the stains on the mattress. Picky, that's me.

On day four, it rained and rained. During the day we walked through white water, grey water and mustard-coloured water, but the worst was the brown water. This was because when we came to the brown water in the late afternoon we had already walked through the white water, the grey water and the mustard-coloured water, and the novelty had really, really worn off. In the morning I had rather enjoyed it. It had reminded me of walking through puddles when I was a kid. The rain dripped off the sweet chestnut trees and made the yellow and green leaves shiny and luminous. Underfoot the ground was thick with sweet chestnuts (the dog had a terrible time with their spines) and we fed wet chestnuts to the donkeys as we walked along. The path wound uphill but we went slowly and my waterproof coat was waterproof, my waterproof trousers were waterproof and at this point my waterproof boots were still waterproof.

Unfortunately, after a couple of hours we left the chestnut forest and dropped down into an evergreen oak forest which led us to the town of Largentière, which was a nightmare. The plan had been to skirt the town and cross the river at a small ford but this was now impossible because the rain had turned the tiny stream into a raging torrent. So, we had to go right through the town in order to cross the bridge in the town centre, along with all the usual traffic to be found at lunchtime in town centres.

Until the 1950s, there were silver mines in Largentière (hence its name). Judging by the cars which overtook us, the population of Largentière nowadays consists of prosperous ex-silver miners who are now elderly or fragile and who have considerable plumbing problems. This is because one out of every three cars that passed us was huge, one was an ambulance and one was a plumber's van. These statistics are pretty reliable because they are not based on a small sample but on the fifty-or-so cars that overtook us over the hour it took us to get through the town, up the hill the opposite side and off the main road. What a relief to turn off, at last.

'What about lunch?' I croaked from the back. 'I can't go on,' I said. 'Here, have some Armagnac: we can't stop in the rain,' they said, and we didn't. I would never have believed I could have walked eight hours without stopping and without lunch, but I did. It was awful. And then there were all the obstacles. At one point, we had to cross a very busy main road. Here Jacques, who was back with friend Henri, held the traffic up in both directions as we scuttled across what seemed like a major north–south motorway. 'After that road it gets better,' said Gilles, but he didn't mention that he'd never had to do the detour before and he didn't actually know the way. As an experiment, we walked along a disused railway line for half an hour before coming out on the road he'd wanted. But then the donkeys baulked at crossing a narrow bridge because the water-level was too high and too noisy, so we had to do another detour. We got back on the right road again and climbed yet another hill and turned off on to a high plateau with a horizontal cross wind and, yes, brown water in the puddles. But these were not ordinary puddles. These were miniature lakes. On a path that was lined by nasty spiky bushes and strewn with nasty spiky stones, and with the rain driving from the left, you couldn't get round them – you just had to go through. In three of the puddles the water came up to mid-calf. So much for the waterproof boots and the waterproof trousers. The waterproof coat had started leaking down the arms, but at least I was better equipped than Suzanne, who was wearing blue jeans which had gone black with water, or Robert, who was carrying an umbrella (not easy to negotiate, with a donkey and a crosswind).

'What about lunch?' I croaked from the back. 'I can't go on,' I said. 'Here, have the last of the Armagnac: we can't stop in the rain,' they said, and we didn't. Valérie and Gilles had a mild discussion as to whether we should have gone straight on back there, or to the left, but I don't think either of them cared. Certainly no one else did. And then we came out on to a road with pretty red-tiled roofs in view. 'Nearly there,' said Gilles, but of course he wasn't talking about those roofs, but the ones further on at a place called Balazuc.

What seemed like hours later we finally got there: an extremely picturesque holiday centre set in stone farm buildings on the banks of the River Ardèche, some 30m below. At the top, as there was no road down, Gilles issued us with our luggage from the van. At this point I keenly regretted not having listened to him that morning when he'd said to make sure our stuff for the night was easy to get at. Mine was in three different bags. Going down fifty-or-so rough stone steps in the dark and the rain, trying to prevent the donkey getting in front without tripping it up with two holdalls and a suitcase with natty little wheels was so horrendous that I finally jettisoned the suitcase. Fortunately, Gilles, being patient and heroic, collected it on his way past and brought it down with him, and we all got to the bottom without mishap. I had never imagined that donkeys could climb down steps but, having seen what they did that evening, it would not now surprise me to learn that donkeys can climb ladders.

At the bottom was a sort of mini-paradise. There was pasture for the donkeys and a warm welcome for us from a wonderful woman called Marie who took our wet things away to tumble dry them. She provided us with salad and rice and *saucisson* and pasta and apples and jam and goat's cheese

and honey and hot showers, all 100 per cent organic and ecologically sound. We had a very pleasant evening, made even
pleasanter by Gilles hinting that if it was still raining in the
morning he would take the donkeys the remainder of the way
by van and then take us home. We all heaved sighs of relief and
went off to bed content to sleep on organic wool mattresses.

Unfortunately, the women's bedroom was tiny and overlooked the River Ardèche which made such a loud rushing
noise in the pitch dark that it drowned the sound of the
pouring rain and kept me awake. I felt as if I were buried in a
stone tomb under a waterfall and didn't sleep a wink. I have
rarely spent such a long and unpleasant sleepless night, despite
the organic wool mattress. I would have willing exchanged it
for a nice foam mattress in a motel at the side of a motorway.

Day five, and much to my disappointment, it had stopped
raining some time in the night, so the trip was on again.
Jacques had come back armed with a video camera, so he
recorded us catching the donkeys, loading them up and
setting off along the river bank to the village. Whiskey had
cut his paws on the spiky stones the previous day and was
obliged to travel in the van with Jacques. He had to be helped
up on to the passenger seat but once installed, looked most
self-satisfied as he watched us plod away. For us walkers, the
day went by in a blur. It didn't rain but it kept threatening to.
We walked up hills and down hills through typical *garrigue*
countryside – spiky vegetation, spiky stones – and at regular
intervals Gilles said 'Nearly there' or 'Last hill coming up'.
We were allowed to stop for lunch that day and filmed each
other eating organic boiled eggs, red wine, *saucisson*, apples
and lots of other organic things. We filmed our lively debate
about organic agriculture. As Jacques was a non-organic
farmer he had plenty to say. He was very indignant about the
fact that he receives the same prices for growing maize now as
he did thirty years ago when he first started farming, and he

considered that non-organic farmers were being taken for a ride by the French government. Then Jacques and Whiskey got back in the van and drove off and we dragged ourselves to our feet, collected our donkeys and set off again.

'Nearly there,' said Gilles. This time we really were very nearly there. At last the path turned definitively downhill. We were so near our destination that we met Jacques, who'd brought Whiskey to meet us as we passed the winter quarters of Gilles' horses. He filmed Gilles running his hands under their bellies to check for ticks. He filmed us walking along, asking us stupid questions like 'What is your donkey called? Are you tired?' Only 200m further on we let the donkeys loose on their hillside and marvelled that we'd made it. He filmed us lying on the grass with our shoes off, gibbering hysterically about how wonderful it had been. We parted company that evening content and full of beer and *camaraderie* after a stop in the village bar where we each explained to the camera which bit we'd liked best and wished each other well.

As always, the drive back to Pradelles was incredibly short – the equivalent of five days' walking took only an hour and a half in the van. But the thing I really do not understand is how, despite the starting point being on a mountain (1150m altitude) and the finishing point on a hill (only 300m altitude), the 100km in between were mainly uphill. And how is it that even in the downhill bits there were lots of hills going up? Downhill all the way indeed!

The itinerary (it would make a lovely walk unencumbered by donkeys):
Day one: Pradelles–Le Bouteirou (12km)
Day two: Le Bouteirou–La Croix de Bauzon (18km)
Day three: La Croix de Bauzon–Chazeaux (27km)
Day four: Chazeaux–Le Vieil Audon, Balazuc (24km)
Day five: Le Vieil Audon–St Maurice d'Ibie (15km)

CHOOSING YOUR COMPANIONS

In which Molly wonders why it is so hard to find
perfect companions (except Hilary, of course)

This is a difficult one as firstly it is not always easy to find companions other than a donkey so you can't be too choosy, but on the other hand the wrong companions can put a damper on the festivities and may spoil your holiday. Purists would argue that only a donkey is required anyway, but I think it is a shame not to have companions with whom to share the happy revelations and minor mishaps of walking the Stevenson Trail. Discovering the wonders of nature and getting lost and getting found are moments which are enhanced by being shared. Also, putting the donkey's pack back on again for the third time the same day tends to be less amusing when it can't be shared.

However, walking for hours and hours in deserted, beautiful countryside allows the primeval nature of each person assert itself. You will come to know the people you travel with much better than you ever did before as they, and you, are pushed to their limits and basic instincts take over, so care is needed.

When selecting companions you should begin with seeking out those who are congenial to you. Given that the Trail is marked out, that bed-and-breakfasts are plentiful, there is not much need to encumber yourself with expert persons with specialised skills, such as scouts, guides and pathfinders, donkey experts or those with mountaineering skills. Common sense, calmness, and a sense of humour make the ordeal – sorry, experience – happier and easier.

You should also keep in mind that you need to be able to

walk along in multiples of two. Even on the Stevenson Trail, three's a crowd. In groups of three, two people tend to gang up and the third person may feel left out. A group of five people is better than three but too much for one donkey unless you carry some of the luggage yourselves. In fact, two or four people per donkey are excellent. Once you get into needing two donkeys you're into a whole new ball game, akin to trekking in the Sahara and you should put this book down immediately and buy a proper guidebook. Couples are to be avoided unless the whole party is made up of couples. It is not a good idea to mix couples and singles and donkeys, as inevitably conflicts will arise. In any case, a strange, childish rivalry tends to emerge concerning who should lead the donkey, who should push it and who should feed it. Compound this with flirting and dallying and there's no telling where it might lead. Take care, then, to share chores and to take it in turns to load the donkey up, feed him, lead him, etc. Otherwise the person who does most will feel put upon, and the others resentful.

You should also choose your donkey with the same care as your human companions. If you are going as a family group with young children, select a calm, steady donkey who will be patient and not streak off over the horizon if you drop his leading rein. Don't let the children lead the donkey to begin with: wait until he has understood that you are boss. Whatever happens, you need to keep an eye on children and donkey – and your wits about you. If not, you may have the same experience as a family who hired Noisette one morning and who returned to Gilles' bar later that afternoon, without even having left the village. They had foolishly assumed that the donkey knew the way and had merely followed her around. If, on the other hand, you are going with a party of intrepid walkers, choose a lively donkey full of get up and go.

In any case, the donkey will add much more to the expedition than just a means of getting your bags from A to B. You will find your perception of the Trail is heightened by including the donkey. You will begin to see things from his point of view, and the countryside will no longer be just decor but a source of delightful discoveries. (For example, 'Oh look, thistles' or 'Big puddle coming up: how can we get round it?')

Walking speeds also need to be taken into account. If you like dawdling, take dawdlers with you; if you like covering a maximum of ground in a minimum time, don't take a donkey (it will slow you down) but select keen, fit people of like mind and take a motorbike instead (no, please do not take a motorbike).

In fact, the key is likemindedness in all senses of the word. You need to *like* the other people and also to *mind* (as in 'mind that lorry') their interests and feelings.

If you can agree on the route as well, your trip is made.

Clive, Florence, Molly and Hilary with Jeep and Whiskey at Le Monastier.

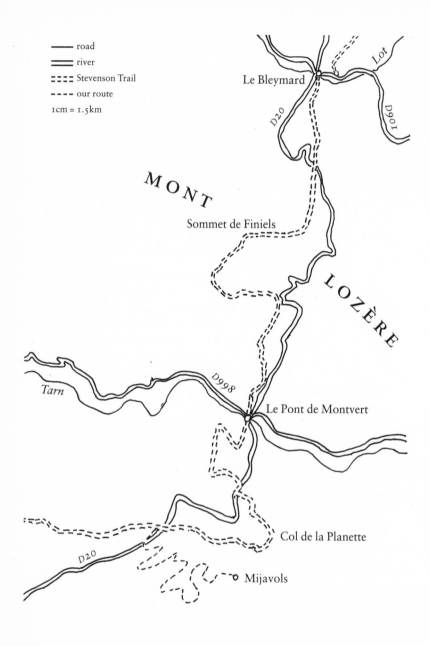

road
river
Stevenson Trail
our route
1cm = 1.5km

Le Bleymard

Lot

D20

D901

M O N T

Sommet de Finiels

L O Z È R E

Tarn

D998

Le Pont de Montvert

Col de la Planette

D20

Mijavols

ALMOST THERE
Le Bleymard–Mijavols

In which Hilary reads the map

I hadn't realised that Molly was so cross with me until she started talking to me again. It was about 3pm on the third day in a very pretty beech grove at Champlong de Bougés. That was just before things got very bad.

This journey had started well, despite the impending doom of Mont Lozère. For a start, I'd got the train to Langogne right in the heart of the Cévennes, cutting out motorway driving in favour of a five-star rail journey. The train from Clermont le Ferrand plunged in and out of darkness – I counted fifty tunnels before Langogne. In between it chugged through cuttings gouged out of rock, past trees slithering down towards the valley floor, across a bridge spanning a deep river far below towering rock faces, occasional pines clinging tenaciously to them, pylons strutting over the top. The less dramatic crevices were filled with swathes of broom, clouds of love-in-the-mist, yards and yards of hedgerow dusted with white blossom. A ginger slender-legged foal staggered to its feet and picked its way carefully after its mother. At Mositrol d'Allier a bunch of walkers dismounted from the train and strode off into the distance. It was May in all its promising glory.

And amid this delight lurked the familiar sense of dread. What was I doing here again? Why was I even contemplating climbing Mont Lozère? Part of me just wanted it to be next Monday when we would have finished the Stevenson Trail and I would be on my way back to my own life. Still, at least I knew we were better prepared than we had been before. This time, my boots had even been sprayed with waterproofer, and

Molly – she'd proudly told me – had invested in a plastic holder for the map.

At Langogne I strolled up and down in front of the station until Gilles' wife Suzanne with their son Bruno arrived in a car, and then, a few minutes later, Molly on foot with Whiskey and a bunch of flowers – cowslips, narcissi, white nettle, hawthorn – which she had picked *en route*. She'd walked from Pradelles. She was in training.

Back at the Brasserie du Musée, a long table had been laid out with *pichets* of wine, plates of cold meat, crusty bread, tomatoes and mozzarella, all to augment the still-steaming pizzas Bruno had picked up in Langogne. The big news of the meal was about Noisette, who, we had been told on our last visit, was missing and presumed dead. No longer. Gilles had seen her. When taking the horses down in the autumn, Gilles had spotted her in a field with other donkeys, a victim of donkey-rustling. '*Certainement, c'était Noisette,*' asserted Gilles. He had called her name, and she had trotted eagerly over to him. The following week he had returned. But the donkey-rustler had come to the door with a gun, a convincing way of asserting his ownership. Gilles had backed off from confrontation, and had relinquished his claim to Noisette. It was still a matter of some melancholy for Gilles.

We were due to start what we thought would be our last push early the next day. Naturally we were late. But we took our time over breakfast, determined to savour it, rather with the attitude of a doomed man before he is hanged. Whiskey certainly enjoyed it. He was showered with attention, petted by the other breakfasters and hankered after by a plump mushroom-coloured poodle. She gazed longingly at him, panting slightly: one of her long ears was trapped in her collar giving her a swept-off-the-face coiffure and alluring look. Whiskey, naturally, took it all as his due.

Down at the donkey field it rather seemed to me that

Kenneth wasn't overjoyed to see us, but he was inveigled into the back of the van. We bowled through the Cévennes, seen in snatches as we rounded bends in the road. Below us, a pancake layer of milky-thick cloud lay at the bottom of the valley with sky of a piercing translucent blue above. Thick clumps of wild mountain daffodils, pale-lemon-coloured and short-stemmed, clustered on the hillside. Two figures, tiny in the depths, tilled a patch of very black earth on the hillside, lining it up into miniature fertile furrows.

At Le Bleymard, we coaxed a reluctant Kenneth out of the van (he obviously knew what he was in for), loaded up the panniers, bade affectionate goodbyes to Gilles, walked into the village and, as was our wont, got lost. It was a source of some wonderment that even after several attempts we found it impossible to either make sense of the guidebook or to detect the red and white markings of the *Grande Randonnée*. How, after all our experience, could we be so hopeless? Eventually, a helpful three-some chatting on a doorstep directed us on to the Trail. And the long-anticipated ordeal began.

There was now no excuse. We had been enormously relieved last September to be excused the ascent of Mont Lozère because of the appalling weather. But there was no way round it now. We just had to climb it.

Steps to the church at Le Bleymard.

We would, we decided, walk for an hour without stopping. To our surprise – this certainly wasn't our usual practice – we managed it easily, pausing just after noon to reward ourselves with a little something. With renewed vigour we strode onwards to the ski centre of Chalet Mont Lozère, where a couple who were out for the day (how very effete!) spotted Kenneth, asked about our exploits, and photographed us for their album. Feeling somehow validated by this recognition, we pressed on and found that by 12:45 we had covered two sections of the guidebook and 5km. This was all rather cheering.

But then the grind began. The first part of the next section up to Mont Lozère was delineated by *montjoies de granite* (like giant fingers of stone), some sharply stabbing upwards, others gently curvaceous, presenting a pleasing vista behind us as they stretched into the distance, marking our progress. Kenneth, in his reassuring way, was unfazed by the gradient, solidly plodding upwards over the scrubby ground, which was unadorned with wild flowers at this height. The going was hard but we could manage this. So I thought at the time. I didn't realise then just how exhausted Molly was.

We turned off to the right, faithfully following, we thought, RLS's steps up to the peak of Mont Lozère. Journey's nadir, I reflected, though a peak couldn't properly be called a nadir. I mulled over the contradiction as we ground up the last few feet. Relief at last . . . until we discovered that the pile of stones here did not mark the summit at all. Molly's dark mumblings, which I had been laughing lightly at, taking them as part of the spirit-lifting banter accompanying the hardest slogs, took on a note of increased intensity. Perhaps she was more serious than I had realised.

We trudged down into a dip and up to another summit, though frankly it did not look any higher to us. But someone somewhere thought it was, which was the important thing: a rather small sign denoted this as Sommet de Finiels, 1699m (5576 feet, in English).

With an overdue sense of achievement we ate our baguettes up there and admired the view. Kenneth, left out of the celebratory feast, found he could reach Whiskey's plastic water bowl, which was strapped to the *bât*, by twisting his head over his right shoulder, and bit a chunk out of it. This was unfortunate for Whiskey (though, as we later left it on a wall, it mattered less than we thought). The couple we had seen earlier came striding up – a mite too energetically for my liking – and took a photo of us at the pinnacle of our success.

'That's the worst of it over,' said Molly. We allowed ourselves to feel exhilarated. It was downhill all the way from here, literally and metaphorically too. There was something to be said for getting the bad stuff out of the way on the first day. The skylarks were trilling and we felt smug, as we took the path south over springy turf past F-I-N-I-E-L-S spelt out in stones. Our route lay down a rocky course like the bed of a stream which Kenneth, with his usual enthusiasm for descent,

Sandwich stop on the top of Mont Lozère.

saw as some sort of macho challenge. He plunged down, practically leaping from boulder to boulder, while we took it in turns – and occasionally joined forces – to lean back on his rope to slow him down. During one of these bouts of attempted deceleration, Molly fell, thumping her knee sharply against a rock. But we remained on a high: we were on the way down.

At the bottom we stopped for a snack by a pond surrounded thickly by golden marsh marigolds. (That was where we left Whiskey's bowl.) We found there were still obstacles to be navigated. The path, which until this point had seemed charming, led to a gate which said politely: 'Cows in Freedom. Please Close the Gate. Thank You.' 'I don't like the sound of that,' said Molly, as she cast constant anxious glances about – cows and donkeys don't mix well – but the grassy-smooth, rock-spattered broom-bright hillside appeared, in fact, to be cow-free. Then there were the stream crossings. The first had a bridge. The second had crossing stones. The third didn't. These were tricky, as we had a donkey who deeply disliked running water.

The first was easy. The second wasn't too bad: Molly, donkey in tow, waded through the shallow water without pause, her feet already wet despite the inner lining of plastic bags. I, still conscious of my carefully waterproofed boots, managed to balance delicately and rather ridiculously on the stones while pushing Kenneth from behind.

The third was a different matter. For a start this stream was more like a river. Kenneth balked at the flowing water, backing away and skittering. Molly splashed through with Whiskey, deposited him on the other bank and then returned to concentrate on Kenneth, talking to him soothingly while firmly pulling his halter. Shoving was also required. This didn't seem quite the time to worry about the waterproofing on my boots.

And so the soggy squelch of wet boots joined the other woodland sounds as we moved in convoy along the mossy path and on to the streets of Le Pont de Montvert, where we ran straight into a traffic jam. Well, perhaps it wouldn't be considered so in London or Montpellier, but after a day of coming across just two walkers and no transport at all, the queue of eight cars was startling.

We could see the Hôtel des Cévennes, where we were headed, on the other side of the thirteenth-century bridge which gives the town its name. As we got closer, it looked charming – aged, mellow, wonky-roofed. There was even a hitching rail. We hitched Kenneth to it and instantly became a tourist attraction. Passing walkers nudged each other and pointed. As Molly went to investigate the hotel, a car pulled up, its driver leapt out and with video camera clamped to eye, fired questions at me in the manner of Jeremy Paxman – Where had I come from? Where was I going? Who was Stevenson? – all the time panning over Kenneth from ears to tail. It was quite disconcerting conversing with someone

The bridge at Le Pont de Montvert.

whose right eye was transformed by a mechanical proboscis. Kenneth, meanwhile, was utterly unconcerned by his moment of stardom.

Molly returned with the blue-aproned *patron* who was to show us where to berth the donkey. He took us past a lovely old archway studded with ferns to the tack room, indicating the buckets, the sack of donkey nuts, the rings to tether Kenneth to while we ministered to him, and the field clinging to the hillside where he would spend the night. It already contained a donkey, the first from another hirer (Badjane, we were told, at Altier, slightly off the Trail) we had come across.

With Kenneth installed for the night, we retreated in relief to our quarters and found a dingy, dimly lit room with a cracked sink and a double bed squeezed into an alcove. It wouldn't do. We made a fuss and were given a room in the annexe across the road. This one had matching pillows, curtains and headboards, and a set of chain-store brown and orange 1920s-style prints on the wall. It was almost welcoming. At least it had separate beds, a decent shower room and a very narrow heater over which we optimistically tried to dry two sets of sodden boots, socks and trousers.

Perhaps it was the view of the river from inside a warm room, or the great bunch of Chinese lanterns mixed with spring flowers, or the stacks of gleaming glass and china on the red-ruffled shelves of the dresser, but the restaurant instantly restored our good humour. Or perhaps it was the supper, which, unlike the accommodation, was excellent: vegetable soup (in our own tureen), lamb in red wine sauce with crispy potatoes, cheese and a plum tart. We drank a *demi-pichet* of good red wine and ended with home-made verbena tea, the leaves stuffed just anyhow into a pot, with boiling water poured over. RLS had eaten here too, but had only considered the 'cow-like' charms of the waitress, Clarisse. For us, however, this meal was one of the highlights of our travels with a donkey.

We woke to the sound of rain, rain of a particularly relentless sort. Molly made a few tentative enquiries of me about staying put. Perhaps I'd like to explore Le Pont de Montvert? Perhaps I'd like to do something else altogether? I thought I wouldn't, but said instead 'Let's think about it after breakfast.' Perhaps the rain would stop. After breakfast, it was still raining. I said 'Let's go for a walk.' We looked at the ancient tower next to the ancient bridge, the source of the bell twice tolling the hours (the second was from the days of people working in the fields, without watches, in case they had not heard the first). We took pictures of the gnarled houses and we shopped: we bought cherries, apples, postcards, *escargots* – whirls of Danish pastry – for our elevenses (even though it was nearly 11:30 by now).

It was still raining.

We went to collect our picnic lunch. There'd been a lot of shouldershrugging and headshaking when we'd asked for this after breakfast. The *patronne* was not pleased. We should have asked yesterday. But she'd relented and made us a huge spread – great hunks of pork between great hunks of bread, with tomatoes, tuna salad, fruitcake, fruit.

It was still raining.

But a bit of resolve would see us through, we were made of stern stuff. I thought. So we prepared for departure. Under a big blue umbrella, the *patron* accompanied us up to the field and volunteered to hold the Badjane donkey while we extricated Kenneth to load him up. Badjane donkey had other ideas, bucking and rearing as though auditioning for a part in a Wild West show. The *patron* eventually jettisoned his umbrella to use both hands on the recalcitrant donkey's halter – whereupon recalcitrant donkey became completely calm. It was the umbrella that had alarmed him. Serene donkey. Soaked *patron*. He was glad to see the back of us.

The Stevenson Trail lay up through this almost vertical field, zigzagging back and forth to the high peak above. Molly, unsuccessful in her attempts to deflect our expedition, was rather quiet. She had been in favour of walking along the – almost level – road. But I insisted upon being purist and sticking to the Trail. I did, however, take charge of Kenneth – only fair, as I was the one insisting on doing it by the book. As I then thought.

Oblivious to the silence behind, my spirits soared. The rain stopped. There was a patch of blue sky – there was even a hint of sun. The path levelled out and led into the shelter of a beech grove at Champlong de Bouges. It was there, as we sat eating our *escargots* and Molly announced she had forgiven me, that I belatedly realised that for the past few kilometres she had not just been silent but simmering with annoyance at my determination to stick to the Trail. Still, all was well now and resting here under newly leafing trees was very pleasant. We briefly basked.

That was the high point of the day. Things went downhill fast after that or, more accurately, uphill. Whatever the guidebook said, whatever the map showed, this hill we were now climbing was much steeper than Mont Lozère. We had to bend double in the effort of mounting it, enough in itself to make us miserable. But what was worse was that, as we were locked in combat with the contours, the rain started again. Not in the mildly determined way of the morning (now we thought about it, that had really been rather agreeable) but in a crashing, tumultuous, drenching downpour. Water drummed down, bouncing off the forest floor. The track ahead was obscured by mist. Thunder cracked and rolled directly overhead; lightning forked vividly and demonically across the sky. We toiled up through woods that seemed to be the site of a recent cyclone – branches and tree trunks strewn wildly across the path. Kenneth's hooves slipped and slid as we negotiated our way round the obstacles. Kenneth wasn't happy. Neither were we. We stopped to eat the remains of the fruitcake. Molly rested her head exhaustedly on Kenneth's flank. We didn't exchange quips. We didn't talk at all.

When we got to the top of Col de la Planette, on the level at last, it should have been easier going. But it wasn't. Exposed as we were, it was much more difficult. It began to hail, large hard lumps striking diagonally, lancing into us. The wind was in full spate, buffeting us as we struggled to keep our balance and the donkey under control. Over and over again, Kenneth turned sideways, trying to get his back into the storm and wind. Even Whiskey – ever cheerful – lost his bounce, trotting miserably behind, tail dipped. Up there, even the beech trees were cowed, clinging low to the ground in an effort to escape the blast and, in this harsh environment, barely in bud.

In an effort to distract ourselves from utter sodden misery, we forced ourselves to look around, catching glimpses of a tree of extreme green – almost neon, as Molly pointed out in a rare communication; silver birch, all lacy; shreds of apple blossom and occasional cherry blossom; the stele at the junction with the *Grande Randonnée 68* in memory of Raymond Senn, who had completed and maintained that footpath (it was people

Despair on the lower slopes of Col de la Planette: Molly and Kenneth.

like him who were to blame for our present predicament, I savagely pointed out); and an inexplicable monument in a clearing of seven or eight towering piles of slate-like flat rocks.

But it didn't work. We reverted to concentrating on surviving the elements. Our boots were soaked through without any help from streams. Occasionally Molly would, pointlessly, stoop to adjust the plastic bags in her boots. Unable to wear her waterproof trousers because her knee was swollen after yesterday's fall, her trousers were wet to her thigh. She was wretched. I retreated inside my cagoule and listened to the insistent beat of the rain on my hood. We stopped from time to time in desperation or to eat cherries, or take a swig from the small bottle of *eau-de-vie* Molly had thoughtfully brought (oh, how prepared we were this time). But most of the time, heads down, unspeaking, we grimly trod on.

The worst was to come. We saw the sign pointing to Mijavols, where we had reserved beds in a *gîte d'étape*. We turned downhill, now facing into the storm, the icy rain stinging our faces, but at least with the thought that we were soon to be at journey's end, for the day at least. But at a swampy T-junction, there was no other signpost. The tracks in opposing directions offered no clue, each looking equally barren. Molly pondered over her map in its plastic case. I looked around hopefully for human life. A foolish hope.

Molly settled on walking left. I pored over the map and thought it should be right. It wasn't easy in those conditions to have an informed discussion about it. In the end, we did go right, following the path that curved round first one hill then another, still with no sign of habitation. My heart began to pound with alarm. How long would we have to walk before we discovered we were on the wrong route? I wasn't sure I could endure Molly's reproof.

Kenneth, fur running with water, was as morose as a donkey could possibly be, and the form his bad humour took was swerving this way and that across the track. We had hardly the strength or the will to deter him, trailing after him with feeble curses. We were wet and fed up, our hands mottled red and blue with cold, our noses numb, our feet weighed down with water, despair in our hearts. The rain, which had slackened off, started up again with renewed intensity. And we still didn't know if we were going the right way. It was a dismal half-hour.

At a junction there was, thank the Lord, a sign to Mijavols. It was only 500m. Such is the resilience of human nature that we perked up immediately. We were so happy! We chattered to each other in relief. The first building we came to was a stone-built house with chimneys like witches' hats, and, wonderfully, smoke coming out of one chimney. It was charming. It was the *gîte d'étape*. We were home and dry, or would be soon.

Of course, that was before we realised that the only heating in the *gîte* was from the fireplace where was lodged a great chunk of tree trunk sullenly glowing at the edges, managing in a quite extraordinarily effective way to emanate neither light nor heat. And before we realised the owner had gone to her sister's 35th wedding anniversary celebration. There was a note on the table for all the residents: '*Rassurez-vous, nous serons de retour ce soir.*'

The meal, said the note, would be 'about 8:30'. Molly, with years of experience of unfulfilled promises in France, was sceptical about an early return from a celebration. But we had Kenneth to worry about, so we freed him of his load and investigated his accommodation. The outhouse, a lean-to laden down with tyres, was dank, smelly and uninviting, so we let him into the field opposite. Chickens pecked around a mountainous pile of manure close to the gate. Beyond that, however, there was a great deal of lush grass. Kenneth took himself off towards it in a rather long-suffering way.

We turned to our own *déchargement*. Already many pairs of trousers and dripping waterproofs were festooned around the miserable fire and suspended from nails in the roof beams.

Rows of boots were lined up near the smouldering wood in obviously hopeless attempt to be dried. We nudged our own saturated garments and boots into prime positions.

Life seemed slightly better in dry clothes (thanks to bin bags) and it was a quaint *gîte*, we agreed, with benches of wood, three-legged carved stools, imposing fireplace, original shepherd's bed built into an alcove. Quaint, but bleak and cold. My nose had not been so cold since January. A sheet of metal leaned against the door to prevent the rain blowing in through the gap beneath. It didn't.

The evening drifted on and the other residents drifted out, doubtless to drive off to comfortable, cheery, cosy bars in nearby towns. We gradually realised we were alone in the *gîte*. At 8:25, with still no sign of supper, we adjourned glumly to the dormitory, which was less draughty, and crouched on the bunks to eat the remains of our tuna salad.

We were wrong to be so pessimistic. Had we read the rules of the *gîte*, we would have seen that meals were served in a house further up the village at the *gîte d'accueil*. That was where the other residents had gone. But we didn't know this until the next day. At 9pm, Molly went to bed with all her clothes on and three extra blankets, purloined from other beds. 'I shan't be doing this again,' she said grimly as she lay rigidly, gazing up at the bunk above.

The next morning we – and no doubt everyone else in the dormitory – were woken by the sound of Whiskey's toenails clicking on the wooden floor as he roamed around waiting for Molly to take him out. When finally she complied, she reported back that Kenneth was still in the meadow – reassuring, she said. But I hadn't heard her properly: 'I thought you said "What a shame." Losing the donkey would at least have been a good excuse to call out Gilles.' It was our regular mantra, our fall-back position: 'We can always phone Gilles and get him to take us back to Pradelles.' Oh, if only we could. . . .

Our boots and waterproofs were still wet when we pulled them on. At 8:15, we found our way to the *gîte d'accueil* – a misnomer, as it was not, despite its name, at all welcoming when we got there. *Gîte*-woman was standing in the middle of the road, arms folded. 'Where are the others? Why aren't they here?' she demanded. 'And where were you last night? Why didn't you come for dinner?' Barely waiting for our response, she led us past a byre full of sheep, eyes glinting green in the gloom, into a large room which ran from front to back of the house, fire at one end (*this* one was blazing), and window at the other. Pride of place among the family photos was the one of her son and a large gun leaning against a truck.

She slammed down not particularly hot coffee and lukewarm milk on the table. Molly asked for hot water instead of milk to go with her hot chocolate. '*C'est compliqué,*' she huffed, as she stomped back into her kitchen.

To make conversation, we mentioned Kenneth, and she asked in sharp alarm. 'Donkey? You have a donkey? Where did you put it? *Mon Dieu!* In the field with the cows? They've probably killed him by now. Did you tie up the gate again?' She had, it seemed, forgotten we'd booked in the donkey along with ourselves.

'Where were we supposed to put it?' asked Molly.

'In the byre.'

'Without food?' asked Molly.

'If you wanted food for the donkey you should have asked when you booked.'

As we left after our meagre breakfast, rather hastily to check on Kenneth's continued wellbeing, she said firmly: 'Make sure you fasten the gate.' 'Of course,' replied Molly, rather witheringly. 'We are sensible people.'

But not that sensible. Or we wouldn't have stayed at Mijavols at all. Just along the road was Les Trois Tilleuls. If only we'd known. . . .

DONKEY PHRASE AND FABLE

In which Hilary tells tales

A donkey driver exhorts his donkey to flee as the enemy closes in. The strangely articulate donkey asks if the enemy would load him with two sets of panniers instead of one. 'No,' said the driver. 'Then,' replies the donkey, 'what care I whether you are my master or some other?' (This attitude was familiar to us: all our donkeys regarded us with equal insouciance – or even disdain.)

This is one of the rare fables attributed to Aesop that conveys a more positive, reflective, image of donkeys. Aesop favoured donkeys above all other animals as a participant in his tales – but mainly, it seems, to show them in a bad light. The donkeys are forever falling into ponds or ditches, being bested by very small animals (such as frogs or grasshoppers) or simply being stupid. The moral to be drawn is that Aesop was deeply prejudiced against donkeys.

Far preferable is the Grimms' fairy tale *The Musician of Bremen*, in which a donkey, in danger of being laid off (or worse) by its owner, enterprisingly decides to run away to Bremen to become a musician, collecting a dog, cat and rooster on the way, with similar ambitions. It is the donkey who provides leadership. It is the donkey who provides the brains of the operation to take over a robbers' house *en route*. This is a donkey with charisma and style.

* * *

Donkeys are credited with the invention of pruning of vines, back in Roman times. Growers noticed that the vines that gave the best fruit were those that had been grazed back by donkeys in the winter and then left alone by them in the spring and summer. The growers followed their example – with results that were good enough for the practice to be continued.

* * *

Donkeys are responsible for another feature of present-day France: a *dos d'âne* is a 'sleeping policeman'.

* * *

Donkey work: what we thought we were doing, rather than the donkey – especially with Noisette. But in Blackpool donkeys giving rides on the beach have workers' rights, as laid down by the Council: they must only work between 10am and 7pm, with an hour for lunch, and have Fridays off.

Kenneth, hard at work, crossing the Nimes–Paris railway line with Véro at La Bastide Puylaurent.

Donkey sanctuary: a haven for donkeys. The Indian Ocean island of Lamu off the coast of Kenya has over 2000 donkeys. No cars are allowed on the island (except for that of the District Commissioner). And one of the main tourist attractions of Lamu is the donkey sanctuary – which, curiously, is run by The Donkey Sanctuary based in Devon.

* * *

Donkey's years: a very long time. Said to be derived from the fact that donkeys have long lives, and you never see a dead donkey (it's true that we didn't) – or, more mundanely, from a reference to donkey's ears, which are very long. Whichever, that's what it means now: for us, it's the equivalent of that wretched time on the ridge above Col de la Planette.

* * *

Drop the dead donkey: a reference to a news item dropped when something more important comes along. Shame! What could be more important? (Also the title of a great comedy television series, screened in 1990–98.)

* * *

Talking the hind legs off a donkey: well, we tried very hard. There's no truth in it though.

* * *

Speaking donkeys: common in Persian literature. The Prophet Mohammad apparently had such a donkey, which he used to summon people. Donkeys are said to bray because they see demons.

Donkey medicine: the old Persian belief was that donkey milk was used to counteract many ailments, including poisons. And a donkey is supposedly useful to have around in the case of a scorpion sting: the pain will be transferred to the unfortunate animal if the victim whispers in its ear or rides facing the tail for seven paces

* * *

An old Tibetan proverb: Engaging in the practice of virtue is as hard as driving a donkey uphill (or, in the case of Kenneth, preventing it from going downhill fast).

* * *

A donkey fell down a well. After failing to find a way of getting it out, the farmer decided to close the well. He asked his neighbours over to help fill the well in. The donkey started to bray when he realised what was happening and then quietened down. After a while, they looked down and were amazed to see that each time they threw shovelfuls of earth on to the donkey's back, he shook it off and climbed up on to the earth he had displaced, thereby, in time, calmly climbing out of the well. It's not recorded what he then did to the farmer, but the moral of this story is: life is going to shovel dirt at you; just shake it off. Whenever nasty things happen to you, do not despair; just turn them to advantage to climb out of your predicament so that you can advance along the Road of Life.

A fitting fable for our progress along the Stevenson Trail.

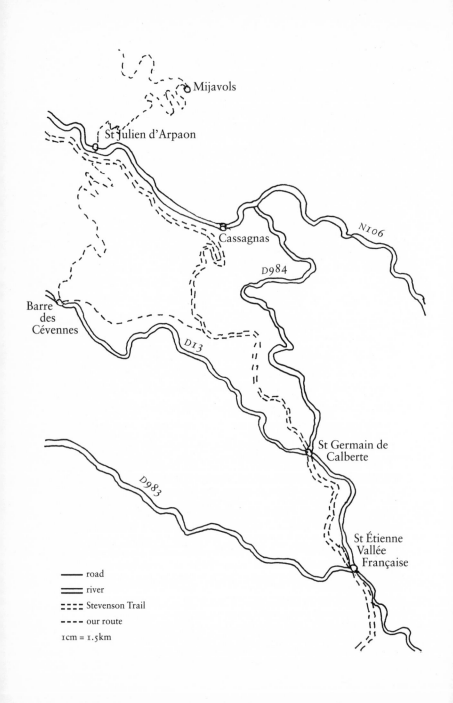

Mijavols

St Julien d'Arpaon

Cassagnas

N106

D984

Barre
des
Cévennes

D13

St Germain de
Calberte

D983

St Étienne
Vallée
Française

——— road
═══ river
▪▪▪▪ Stevenson Trail
▪ ▪ ▪ our route
1cm = 1.5km

LAST LEGS
Mijavols–St Étienne Vallée Française

In which Hilary needs help with a sparrow

We could have stayed at Les Trois Tilleuls. If only we had been better prepared. Even now, on our fourth expedition we were getting things wrong.

After our bad experience at Mijavols, we had determined to reward ourselves with coffee at St Julien d'Arpaon, the next dot on the map. The thought sustained us all the way there. We were still wet, but we were almost cheerful: it wasn't raining; Kenneth had survived his night with the cows and was in a better mood; we were entering new territory with the prospect of cafes and bars unlimited spreading before us. We would, we thought, stop at every opportunity. Food and drink: the punctuation of our ordeal.

But there was no cafe, no bar. It just wasn't that sort of place. A ruined tower on a hill, a bridge, and a few houses strung out along the N106. But there was a *gîte* and *auberge* rolled into one. Les Trois Tilleuls was charming – a scattering of cottages around a central garden, with rowan trees as well as limes, a clean and bright bar. We could see this from peering in the window. Clean, bright and closed.

Molly wasn't putting up with that. Still rankled by the Mijavols misanthrope, she sought out the owner, a smooth-cheeked and amiable young man, and talked him into opening up the bar for us. On the counter was a rack of this year's Stevenson Trail booklets. Les Trois Tilleuls was in, and the *gîte* at Mijavols was out. If only we'd known. . . .

Our new hero cheerfully dispensed coffee and advice on the route. He bent over the map with Molly and indicated the footpath. Molly was attentive – yes, up the hill here, a mountain-top there, and down to cross the stream, alongside for a while and then up a very steep bit to join the path there, and round the woods, there. '*Bien sûr. Je vois. Merci,*' she said. And when we left, she said steelily, as she untethered Kenneth from his rowan tree, 'We will be taking the road. Won't we?'

Yes. Well, I could hardly demur. Last night Molly had read in the *Journal de Route en Cévennes*, the original text of the diary from which *Travels with a Donkey* was taken (we had bought a copy at Hôtel des Cévennes), that RLS had not zigzagged half way up a mountainside as we had done on the way out of Le Pont de Montvert. That was an invention of the Stevenson Trail consortium, not of RLS himself. My purism had been utterly misplaced.

Besides, it was irrelevant too. We were sticking to neither RLS's route nor the Stevenson Trail today. Because it was a Bank Holiday weekend, Molly had been unable to find rooms *en route* for the next stage: Florac was full. Our journey was beginning to resemble a donkey's hind leg as we tacked back and forth across the Trail.

Anyway, this was a very picturesque road. The lower part was fringed with irises, and then it wiggled back and forth upwards under beeches and chestnuts and pretty silvery grey-leafed trees in full bloom with clusters of cream flowers. Higher up, the trees changed from deciduous to coniferous, as the road threaded its way through a thick pine forest.

We climbed steadily and pleasantly up and up to the barer moorland and were soon looking down on the tops of trees. How different from the other day – was it only yesterday? – when we had struggled over the heights of Col de la Planette. We had no picnic lunch (although our hero had wanted to help out, he had no spare provisions) but Molly had a supply of cereal bars and little foil packets of honey. So we had snack stops whenever we came across a field of flowers.

We were alone. In the first 8km we came across one car and one stray dog. All the more shocking then when, close to our goal, we suddenly encountered a stream of traffic: a cavalcade of twenty-nine motorbikes, roaring past, one after another. We stopped for Kenneth's sake, standing on either side of his head. In truth he seemed a good deal less disturbed than we were. Really what was surprising was that, jolted yet again into reality, we could feel, and be, so remote for such long periods of time in such a busy world.

The motorbikes had come from the town we were heading for. After the last couple of days of isolation, Barre des Cévennes seemed to us like a real metropolis. We clopped into town, marvelling at the sights: the restaurant on the outskirts, a Romanesque church in the throes of renovation, shops and a long, narrow, high-housed street. Most importantly of all there was a bar. And a handy drainpipe on the opposite side of the road, just right for hitching donkeys to. A man from the bar helpfully moved his car so to that we could park Kenneth. Molly, with unusually scant regard for Kenneth's comfort, tied him up with great haste. By the time I got to the bar, she was already sitting at a table with a beer in front of her.

This was what we had been fantasising about for the last couple of days. Well, up to a point. It was snug and welcoming, with a buzz of chatter, a womb-like cavern with stone walls, polished silver cups on high shelves, table football – and spread over one wall an orange-red flag with what Molly said was the old fleur-de-lys. 'I think they vote *Front National* round here,' she murmured.

I looked at the half a dozen people in the bar curiously, as if I could decipher their political allegiance from their appearance. There was Serge, who had moved the car – big-shouldered, brown-bearded, drinking pastis – and his blonde girlfriend, drinking brandy. They looked ordinary enough. A man – very pale, with lank grey hair tied back into a limp ponytail – stopped by our table to pick up his plastic bag of shopping and, on his way out, stopped to talk to Serge's girlfriend, saying, conversationally, that he thought he would blow his brains out. Serge's girlfriend listened to him intently: 'If you feel you must, then do, but think about your son,' she counselled. They were still deep in *weltschmerz* when we left.

We took to the road again, savouring the simple attributes of civilisation which we had been deprived of for three days. A *crêperie*! An *épicerie*! A *boulangerie*! Even though it was now nearly teatime, I rushed in and bought lunch – quiche and pizza, sausage rolls and cakes.

The *gîte*, on the edge of the village, seemed to consist mainly of a huge field dotted about by caravans – a ghastly prospect in this wintry weather. But there was also a real building and a welcoming young woman . . . who could find no trace of our booking. 'The name is Wood,' said Molly desperately. 'Whiskey, Omega, Omega, Delta. Wood. *Deux. Et un chien. Et un âne.*'

'We'll find a solution,' said the woman merrily. 'Meanwhile, go and warm up.'

And we did. Cavalierly abandoning Kenneth for the moment, we went into the room with the yellow door, as instructed. Here was a huge proper log fire, with several logs laid neatly this way and that so that it could blaze, unlike the sullenly smouldering lump of tree of yesterday. Joyfully, we unpacked the panniers and stripped off wet jackets, wet hats, wet boots, wet socks and draped them all around the fire. One other individual was crouching by the fire, a motorcyclist. He would have been Number 30 in the cavalcade we had met, but he had woken with a chill. He had, he said, been sleeping in one of the caravans.

The *patronne* came back and said she had found a solution: would we like a caravan or beds on the mezzanine? 'Mezzanine,' said Molly firmly. Look what had happened to the motor-

cyclist: he really did not look well. And so we were led up a thir-
teen-step ladder to an attic where there were camp beds scattered about under the eaves. We chose beds in the part furthest
from the trapdoor opening, and Molly rushed round the room
collecting all the blankets and piling them on her bed. Then,
revitalised, she sorted out Kenneth's night quarters in a cosy
stable with a manger stuffed with hay. I stuck close to the fire.

Around 6pm, the room began to fill up with cyclists in
Lycra shorts, and motorcyclists, large and leathered and loud.
Soon the mantelpiece and hearth were full of and surrounded
by black helmets and buckled boots and leather gauntlets
hanging pendulously down. The jovial crowd played cards,
drank tea out of pots without lids and poured aperitifs into
plastic cups. The ailing motorcyclist offered us whisky and we
drank it and went red in the face.

Kenneth warm and cosy for the night at Barre des Cévennes.

All we needed now was food. We became anxious, thinking that the motorcyclists, who were obviously self-catering, would have to get through their meal before we could eat – activities were beginning at the sink and stoves in the corner. But then the kitchen door in the centre opened and we were summoned to the equally large room on the other side of the kitchen, its long tables covered with yellow plastic fruity-patterned cloths. There we were served a seven-course meal.

There was potato-thickened vegetable soup (several tureens' worth), small dishes of *charcuterie* and olives, a delightful light omelette to cut into sections, a dish of wild boar and mushrooms with boiled potatoes and a platter of ham with chicken sauce in the centre. Then cheese – three sorts – and finally apple tart. All the while baskets of bread – to wipe the plates between courses – and plain glass bottles of wine kept coming.

On one side of us were three delicate Oriental women (from Marseilles, Toulouse and La Réunion, we later discovered) talking quietly together, taking delicate portions and sips of wine. On the other side of us were the cyclists, who wolfed all their meals down and then demanded our leftovers and those of our neighbours and roared and joked and japed. They'd been 45km, so perhaps they deserved it. (The motorcyclists had been 150km. We had been 14km.)

Eventually overwhelmed by the bonhomie of the cyclists, we left the dining room and edged our way back through the common room now overflowing with motorcyclists who seemed to have somehow increased in stature and number. To get to our bathroom we had to go through a dormitory full of male cyclists who thought this a very jolly wheeze. (Molly said the *patronne* had asked if we would like to share with the cyclists because there were two spare beds there, but she had politely declined.)

We went to bed, but not to sleep. An overspill of motorcyclists came up at midnight, chuckling and stumbling – and probably looking for blankets. I spent much of the night awake and wriggling, feeling like a caterpillar in a cocoon or a sausage in its skin. (That's the problem with sheet sleeping bags.) When I did finally sleep, I had a vivid dream about a sparrow being trapped under my coat and I was asking for help to get it out. 'Listen, can't you hear it?' I kept saying. As I gradually surfaced, I realised there really was a sparrow – on the roof, only inches above my nose, infiltrating my dreams.

So well fed but not well slept, we crawled out of bed and set about preparations for another day on the road. Breakfast here – unlike yesterday's – cheered us up a bit. Perhaps it was the home-made jams: rosehip and blackberry. Or perhaps it was that it was not at all '*compliqué*' to have hot water for the hot chocolate.

Outside, the yard was full of cyclists mending punctures, inflating inner tubes, testing them in the puddles and complaining about the cold. Our socks were still not dry. But we were hatted, gloved, packed and ready to go by 9:15. Since the *gîte* was on the road for St Germain de Calbert, we would not get lost; not, at least, to start with. And, another bonus, it soon became clear that this was going to be a better day. The temperature rose, the gradient lessened, the kilometre posts came and went more swiftly.

For the first time in days, the sun came out. We stripped off outer garments in this unfamiliar weather and felt the sun warm on our backs. Kenneth looked happier, with a sleek and neatly furry air, and we were back on the Stevenson Trail. In our heightened sense of enjoyment, we fancied it was just as RLS might have found it. Well, perhaps not entirely. At the crossroads for the Plan de Fontmort, with its obelisk in memory of the Camisards, the Protestant martyrs to whom RLS devotes much discussion, we had one of those Piccadilly

Circus moments as a car *and* a van came along at the same time. The occupants of both stopped to take photos of us. RLS is not in as many photos as we are.

We went off track to find the prehistoric grave indicated by the side of the path and discovered the exact rocky outcrop shown in the picture on the front of the guidebook, *Le Chemin de Stevenson*. It was a eureka moment. We felt as pleased as RLS might have done when he woke in the pine forest to see the dawn breaking: 'a broad streak of orange melting into gold along the mountain-tops of Vivarais. A solemn glee possessed my mind at this gradual and lovely coming in of the day... Nothing had altered but the light, and that, indeed, shed over all a spirit of life and of breathing peace, and moved me to a strange exhilaration.'

Perhaps we were not quite so transported, but we were very pleased. We took several pictures, first with Molly posing as guidebook model posing as RLS gazing soulfully, and then of me, and of course of Kenneth posing as guidebook donkey posing as Modestine. And then we sat and gaped at the view,

Clède, *traditional stone hut in the woods above St Germain de Calberte.*

at the range after range of mountains rippling into the soft horizon, before rousing ourselves to tramp onwards.

Today we had no snack stops. We had several lunch stops instead. The picnic we had been given was big enough for that: crisps and chocolate and oranges, as well as several ham and cheese baguettes. And we were happy. Towards the middle of the afternoon Molly said 'I don't regret coming on the Trail again.' It wasn't a huge endorsement, but it was the first time in four days that either of us had expressed any enjoyment while walking.

'I've learned something from all this,' Molly added. 'To buy new boots. Not to skimp on details. And perseverance. If we hadn't had that, we wouldn't have had such a nice day today.' We'd also learned to be philosophical.

It was indeed an excellent day. The going was good, over carpets of fragrant pine needles or along escarpments with views of rough tussocky green hills rising to rounded distant ranges, multi-layered in each direction. We were in a mood to be charmed by everything: the woods of chestnuts that had provided a living for generations; the stretches of rocky pavement, iridescent, rippled like sand on a drifted beach; our powers of endurance.

Molly was expansive, recounting the fruits of her learning on the *Brevet Professionel Agricole* course she had been doing. She pointed out that the ball of *papier mâché* we could see on a pine tree was the nest of a poisonous caterpillar. She instructed me in the curious reproduction methods of the fig and the best way to cook acacia flowers. This was the Trail as it should be walked.

We began to notice plenty of signposts for *sentiers decouverts*. 'For feeble people who just go for afternoon walks,' said Molly with scorn. 'Armchair walkers. Not like us.'

Still, hardiness has its limits. That morning Molly had switched our reservation at Le Petit Calbertois complex

('equestrian and walking excursions') in St Germain de
Calbert from the *gîte* to the hotel. After the last few nights
what we were in desperate need of was a spot of luxury.

We guessed we were getting near Le Petit Calbertois when
we came to a field with three horses – two white, and one
dappled grey with a long fringe flopping rakishly over one
eye. All together they strolled over to get a better view of
Kenneth, and then escorted us along the fence as far as they
could go (Kenneth took it all in his stride). They stood watching us as we took the track to Le Petit Calbertois, a massive
complex of *gîte*, cottages and hotel, with under-tree tennis
table, swimming pool and a block of stables. The architecture
wasn't pretty – consisting mainly of concrete – but it repre-
sented civilisation and we were beginning to anticipate the
evening with pleasure.

Alicia, the ten-year-old daughter of the *patron*, led us to the
stable block where a young man with cropped hair took
Kenneth off our hands to feed and water him. That was a
good moment.

Then we were led upstairs to a curvy-walled bedroom with
a double bed and bunk beds, all bright in blues and yellows,
with a balcony, and hot radiator, hot water, hot showers. That
was an even better moment.

Especially for Molly, who disclosed that she'd been
wearing the same clothes for three days, day and night. We
revelled in the common or garden pleasures of life: of taking
off and finally drying damp socks, of being clean, of taking
tea on the terrace in the sun, and of a meal in the grand
restaurant with its wall of windows, mountain views, log fire
and scores of lamps (though, truth to tell, the actual food was
not a patch on yesterday's).

It was probably inevitable that the luxury of sleeping
between crisp sheets followed by a basking warm morning
would slow us down. It was mid-morning before we collected

Kenneth, looking very lovely in his brushed brown fur coat, and ambled down the pleasant path through woods and over rocky escarpments to St Germain de Calberte, with its pollarded plane trees, roses rambling over fences and rhododendron bushes in gardens.

This was a scene of strife between Catholics and Camisards in the eighteenth century, as RLS recounts, but this is not commemorated. Instead, in the centre was a statue of a naked man lifting one of a pile of stones, erected in 1995 in homage to the 'Cévennols who had built the Cévennes'. A coachload of tourists arrived from Nîmes and we became part of the scenery as they pointed their cameras at us. Just like RLS. Well, almost: 'Boys followed me a great way off, like a timid sort of lion-hunters; and people turned round to have a second look, or came out of their houses, as I went by. My passage was the first event, you would have fancied, since the Camisards.'

He was eager to move on: their attention 'wearied my spirits'. We, on the other hand, found more excuses to

Looking back to Saint Germain de Calberte.

linger – a bakery (we bought chocolate éclairs) and a fascinating shop in which we spent twenty minutes. Actually it
was just an ordinary village shop, but after five days on the
Trail we were deprived consumers. The clock struck twelve
as we left the village. This was taking us much too long, but
it was hard to get worked up about it on such a beautiful
day. We put on sunhats and suncream, turned our faces up
to the sun and stopped at the river to let Whiskey prance
about in the water.

The air smelled hot and fragrant as we passed hives under
the trees, hearing the background heavy hum. Sun struck
through branches, stippling the ground. Stone buildings with
unevenly tiled roofs clustered together. We met one walker,
elderly and quavery but nevertheless, for a reason we didn't
quite fathom, climbing over his fence which he said was there
to keep wild boar out.

We started hallucinating about foaming pints of beer again
and as we approached St Étienne Vallée Française, we cast
about anxiously, remembering another time when we were
desperate for beer, at St Flour de Mercoire. But here we found
Les Tilleuls, with a terrace full of bamboo chairs shaded by
lime trees, to one of which we tethered Kenneth. 'Ah, Modestine!' said one of a group of walkers passing by. Though we
had not met many who actually followed in the footsteps of
RLS, he certainly had an enduring reputation here.

For the two of us, this turned out to be the end. We
checked the time, examined the map, measured the contours (very close) and calculated how long it would take to
reach St Jean du Gard. Finally we consulted *Travels with a
Donkey* and discovered that RLS allocated few sentences to
this last bit. It would have to wait. In a symbolic gesture,
Molly took off her leaky boots, tied the laces neatly
together and ceremonially dumped them in a dustbin. Time
to call Gilles.

DONKEY FACTS AND FIGURES

In which Molly tests your DAQ (Donkey Awareness Quotient)

Did you know that not all donkeys have crosses on their backs? For example, the Grand Noir du Berry. Only breeds originating in Palestine have crosses.

Did you know that Miniature Mediterranean donkeys (from Sardinia) have pink eyes and stand only 80cm high at the shoulder?

Did you know that donkeys were used by shepherds in Provence in olden times to protect their sheep from bands of ravaging wolves? (This could explain why Jeep, a true-bred *âne de Provence*, didn't like Whiskey – despite the fact that Whiskey, being a Labrador, hasn't got pointy ears and is the wrong colour for a wolf.)

Did you know that the Baudet donkeys of Poitou have long, shaggy, unkempt fur hanging down in ringlets like Orthodox Jews (or droopy rastas) and the longer and shaggier and more unkempt their fur is, the more prized the animal.

Did you know that there are only 400 Baudet donkeys left in the world? They are making a comeback for rather negative reasons as they are used

A rare Baudet de Poitou donkey.

to produce mules for pulling things around in war-stricken areas, and at the moment there is a constant demand.

Did you know that donkeys are more intelligent than horses? This nugget of information comes from a man who pulls felled trees through forests using mules (which, you may point out, are not donkeys, only half-donkeys). He says that before they begin pulling, they will turn around and have a look at the tree trunk in question, in order to assess how much effort to put into it. Horses don't do this, he says, they just pull.

Did you know that some donkeys are black and as big as a horse? For example, the Mammoth Jackstock, though not all donkeys of this breed are black.

Did you know that a hinny is the offspring of a male horse and a female donkey and it is not the same thing as a mule, which is the result of passion between a male donkey and a female horse? The difference is merely terminological, not technical. In French there is one word for both, but then French has a lot fewer words than English, which French people have to compensate for by talking very fast and waving their hands around a lot.

Did you know that you can cross a donkey with a zebra and that the result is a donkey with stripy legs but which is sterile? And speaking of zebras, did you know that the word for zebra in Swahili is *punda milia*, which literally means 'striped donkey'?

Did you know a male donkey is known as a 'jack' and a female as a 'jennet'?

Did you know that donkeys are more economical than horses? For an equivalent-sized animal, they eat less and need less protein. They are also cheaper to buy.

Did you know that if you over-feed your donkey, it will get rolls of fat on its neck (of all places) and on the hips (well, we all know about that) and if the neck roll gets too big it (the neck roll) will fall over to one side and never come back up again? How embarrassing: at least we can go on diets or have lipo-suction but imagine how the donkey feels, carrying a great roll of fat on one side of its neck for ever and ever just because in a period of distress it overdid the cream cakes.

Did you know that donkeys are among the biggest benefi-ciaries of charities in England? Apparently English people find donkeys charming and cuddly. The ones we met cer-tainly were, except perhaps Lulu, who used to sneak up behind other donkeys and wallop them with his front legs, and Eugénie, who nipped Florence when her back was turned, and . . .

Houses huddled together in Le Pont de Montvert.

FINISHING PROPERLY: RETURN TO NOTRE DAME DES NEIGES

In which Hilary is surprised at Matins

Leaning against a tree at Notre Dame des Neiges, silhouetted in the deepening gloom, was the figure of a woman. She was gazing across the valley – as I was – at the peak of Mont Lozère, which had been the symbol of our struggle, but now smoothed about with rose-red clouds. Perhaps she was here on retreat. Perhaps, like me, she had returned with a sense of unfinished business. Perhaps she was just passing through.

RLS had passed through Notre Dame des Neiges, the not entirely silent Trappist monks leaving a profound impression on him as he defended his Protestantism. Despite reaching fame through *Travels with a Donkey*, Notre Dame is not directly on the main Stevenson Trail, though it still puts up donkeys and people – but not dogs. We hadn't stayed here, and this omission had bothered me. On this visit to the Cévennes, we didn't have a donkey but we still had a dog. So while I had booked in here, Molly and Whiskey had to stay in La Bastide Puylaurent, at Michel's hotel. Michel, it turned out, was a changed man from the somnolent and rather lonely couch potato we had previously met. Then he had been planning to join the ranks of donkey bed-and-breakfasters. But he had had a radical rethink: the future was quadbikes! There they were, a score or more, lined up outside the violet-shuttered hotel. Molly and I had met him before we had climbed up to Notre Dame – he'd just come back from a jaunt with some of his guests, bikers from Clermont Ferrand. Muddy-legged and revitalised, he had the confident air of a man who had found his vocation.

On our arrival at the mountain-top monastery in the late afternoon, we'd made a beeline to the heart of the complex of buildings – the shop. This was the centre of a web of gourmet enterprise, selling wine, honey, cheeses and herbs for *tisanes*. The shop had changed out of all recognition since our last visit on a damp autumn day many months before, when we had been fortified with hot chocolate and liqueurs at the dark wooden bar running along one wall. The bar was gone (merely banished to another building, I found later). This was now a shrine devoted entirely to commerce, but commerce with a France-wide religious connection. There was chocolate made by the monks of Bonneville, jam from Grande Trappe, honey from Notre Dame (raspberry, chestnut, and pine) and a wall racked with the different wines made at this monastery and stored in the cellars. The shop assistants were monks, in their white robes and brown cowls. One – unusually young – sat behind the cash register engaged in calligraphy.

I was here, though, for more spiritual matters as well: an almost full hand of religious offices starting with Vespers at 6pm, after Molly and Whiskey had departed, through Compline (8pm) to Laudes (7am). The real challenge would be Matins at 4am. It almost seemed hardly worth taking a bedroom for the night.

But I had: a sparely furnished lino-floored room in the *maison de retraite*. The suitably old-fashioned decor of brownish checked wallpaper and lilac candlewick bedspread was completed by green Provençal print curtains over window and wardrobe. There was, as one would expect in this place of godliness, copious hot water and a big serviceable bar of soap; and starchy clean sheets were dropped on to my bed by the monk who showed me to my quarters.

I managed, true to form, to be late for supper. My guardian monk, with a tight, abstracted smile, was hovering outside the dining room ready to usher me to the furthest table: the other residents were already in place. A Mozart piano concerto was playing: lying beside the cassette player was a book of 'prayers with meals', unopened tonight. I was on the liveliest table, the other two dignified and decorous by comparison, and sitting between two groups of three walkers, both on the Stevenson Trail but *'sans ânes'*. I muscled into the conversation, insisting on telling them about our exploits with donkeys. They for their part were united in a hymn of praise for the Refuge du Moure at Cheylard l'Évêque, which Molly and I had found so uncongenial. Such a find! The food! Out of this world! I retreated into a judicious silence.

Supper here was frugal: thin vegetable soup in a large glass bowl; tasty lasagne in modest portions; a slice of bread each; apples and foil-wrapped apricot cakes for dessert, arranged on a plate which was standing on a covered plastic cheeseboard with four good local cheeses. A no-nonsense unlabelled bottle of red wine in the centre of each table. Everything was served and eaten briskly, except in our group. When the diners at the next table departed, my sharp-eyed neighbour noticed they'd left most of their wine and so, swiftly, switched bottles. We had a hugely convivial meal. But eventually infected by the hustle and bustle of the other residents, the to-ing and fro-ing with dishcloths and water jugs, the clattering of crockery being laid for breakfast, we were shamed into compliance. It was only when I left that I saw the large sign saying that meals were to be taken in silence.

On my way out, I managed at last to find out about payment by waylaying a monk, hitherto monopolised by two nuns engaged in earnest conversation. *'Vingt-cinq euros,'* he said briskly, eager to return to his *tête-a-tête*. *'Les mettre dans la boîte là-bas,'* pointing at a big oaken chest with a slit.

It didn't seem a lot for dinner, bed and breakfast and a chance of salvation.

The life of the monks revolves around prayer, but they are not idle in between. The corridor to the church was lined with antique black-and-white photographs of different activities – working in the fields, with bees, in the library – captioned by quotations from Teilhard de Chardin, Pascal, Pope John XXIII. The focus of their devotions, the modest statue of the Virgin Mary, stood in the porch flanked by a rank of votive lamps and a book filled with prayer requests for world peace, for sick family members, to have children.

The life of the visitors does not revolve around prayer. At Vespers, there had been twenty-eight in the congregation, at Compline after supper, fourteen. At Matins, at 4am, there was one – me. A nun was there briefly but left. I'd even managed to be early, determined to get my money's worth of spiritual experience. I'd arrived before the brothers. Gradually, like a drama unfolding, the monks gathered from different entrances, one from the double doors to the right, another materialising from a side altar, a file of brothers from the archway to the left. As I sat in the centre of the pews roped-off from the faraway altar surveying the scene, I noticed a table skirted in purple that I didn't remember seeing the evening before, with a tall candle burning next to it. As the singing soared, sundry voices piecing together the psalms, my eyes wandered around the simple lines of the church, past the plainness of the altar, returning always to that candle-lit table swathed in purple silk directly in my distant line of vision. What could it be for?

Then gradually, as I stared, my eyes made sense of it, teasing through the optical illusion. The fancy came to me that what I was seeing, from a misleading perspective, was actually a bier draped with the colour of mourning. I couldn't quite believe it. Was I suffering from an over-active imagination? I shuffled sideways to the end of my pew so that I could see it from a different angle, and, yes, that was what it most certainly was: an open coffin, the contours of a body rising above. A monk had died in the night and had been laid out in the church. As Matins came to an end, monks sprinkled holy water from a bowl at the foot of the bier or stood in silent prayer for a few moments. I stayed for a while, mesmerised.

When I left, it was still dark. I went to the dining room and helped myself to a bowl of hot black coffee from the urn. As I stood outside, my hands curled round the bowl for warmth, the birdsong began: a chaffinch perched on the stone gatepost of the *maison de retraite*, sang its heart out as the light grew and grew. Finally the sun burst forth over the peaks, laying long bars of light brilliantly across the grass in a spectacular reminder of the glory of life. It was time for Laudes.

At Matins I had marvelled at the music resonating and rising into the white curves of the ceiling. At Laudes it was the light, inside and out, golden from the lamps or streaming through the stained glass windows, the primary colours falling in abstract shapes on the white. The Mass following Laudes was concelebrated by almost all of the monks together, filing up from the stalls to form a semicircle on the altar. The dividing rope bisecting the church was looped back and the congregation, about twelve this morning, was invited to communion. Moving nearer, I caught a closer glimpse of the bier and the monk. He was dressed in white, with his arms resting on his chest, a grey cap on dark hair, a grey complexion and a drawn and suffering expression. Peace at the end of a life of devotion? It was oddly disturbing.

Moments later, I emerged into bright sunlight to see Whiskey tied to a railing and then, coming round the corner of the abbey, Molly. She too had risen early on this brilliant day and had come to look for me. I took her in to breakfast where we had baguettes spread with *miel de sapin* from Notre Dame's hives. After saying goodbye to my guardian monk, who finally smiled at me slightly less abstractedly, Molly and I strode off together down the mountain. In the distance we could hear and then see a line of quadbikes mounting a track on the other side of the valley, a parade of noisy insects. We were back in the real world, back on the Trail.

Church at Notre Dame des Neiges.

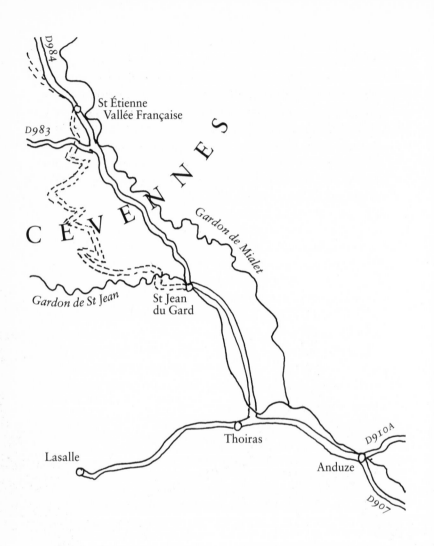

D984

St Étienne
Vallée Française

D983

C É V E N N E S

Gardon de Mialet

Gardon de St Jean

St Jean
du Gard

Thoiras

D910A

Lasalle

Anduze

D907

——— road
═══ river
▪▪▪▪ Stevenson Trail
1cm = 1.5km

LAST STEPS
St Étienne Vallée Française–St Jean du Gard

In which Molly reads the map

On a Sunday in February I was sitting quietly reading in the garden when I was suddenly aware of an evocative combination of birdsong, sunshine and dampness, and it came to me with overwhelming certainty that the time had come to finish the Stevenson Trail. Only 11.5km of the Trail remained untrodden by our eager (and sometimes blistered) feet, representing a mere thumbnail on a map. This was the distance between St Étienne Vallée Française and St Jean du Gard, where Stevenson sold his donkey, leapt into a coach and finished his trip in an unseemly rush to Alès to catch up with his post.

As Hilary was miles away in England and I had no donkey to hand, the first thing to do was to find someone to walk with. In fact this was easy: Véro and Dany, both Stevenson Trail veterans, were keen and Michèle, a friend I'd met through swimming, was fit and an experienced walker.

The day before our expedition, the weather forecast was bad: cold, with either rain or snow according to which TV channel you tuned in to. It was so bad that Dany (who is usually very optimistic) uncharacteristically suggested we postpone the trip until later in the year when it would be warmer and nicer. Equally uncharacteristically (I am usually very pessimistic) I insisted that all would be well.

In a complicated series of manoeuvres involving a cavalcade of three cars (parking two of them in St Jean du Gard), we arrived at our starting point. *En route* I noted with apprehension the thick ground frost and frozen vegetation on the shady side of the hills and reflected dubiously on the previous day's conversation with Dany. Perhaps we should have waited until the weather was warmer.

It was a quarter to twelve when we finally left the car at St Étienne Vallée Française (outside the same bar where Hilary and I had drunk our last beers and opposite the same dustbin where my walking boots met their end the previous spring). Dany explained that, being female, she was hopeless with maps. 'Don't worry,' I said. 'I am female but I am very good with maps,' completely forgetting that Hilary and I would still be wandering around somewhere around Col de la Planette if Hilary had not taken the map away from me and looked at it properly that dreadful day when we got lost in the rain and the hail.

As if to illustrate this, we then couldn't find the Stevenson Trail out of the village and had to go along the road for twenty minutes or so, despite the fact that the Trail was clearly marked on the map as going off to the right and there was a path going off to the right. However, the path in question was marked with yellow markers and Michèle, who knows about these things, told us that all *Grande Randonnées* or GRs are marked with red and white and so the Stevenson Trail, being part of GR70, should also be marked in this way. Since Véro and I could remember it being marked in red and white on an earlier section of the Trail we were convinced, so we played safe and went by the road. It was a small, quiet road that fortunately joined the Stevenson Trail a little further along. This time when the Trail forked off to the right, it was flanked with trees with red-and-white markers, and a picture of a donkey for good measure, so we all agreed to go up it.

Up was the operative word. I was getting nervous about Dany's reaction to the cold (there was still the same thick ground frost and frozen vegetation that we had seen from the car) but the hill was so steep we were soon stripping off coats, hats, scarves, gloves. Soon the only sound to be heard was rasping breathing noises and low, intermittent moans of 'my legs', 'my lungs', 'my feet', 'my cholesterol' – this last from Michèle who, being fit, was the only one who had enough breath to explain in great length about the injustice of being stricken with cholesterol after years of seriously depriving herself of all decent food, eating plain pasta every evening (without butter, cheese or sauce), taking lots of exercise and eating the latest cholesterol-lowering butter substitute. It seems her diet is so limited by cholesterol elim-ination that she sometimes weeps when she contemplates her breakfast.

The path was not only steep but also covered in loose shale in very pretty shades of blue-grey and brown, and I would rather have liked the time to admire it better, but on and on and up and up we went. We all regretted the absence of Kenneth – a day's supply of water and food for myself and Whiskey, emergency rations for four (my normal pessimism kicking in), a change of clothing, a sun hat, a woolly bonnet, waterproof trousers and, in Véro's case, a sheaf of letters to post which she had inadvertently left in her rucksack, weigh a lot. We looked back to those halcyon days when Kenneth carried all those things and much, much more, in those won-derful big leather packs he carried in that wonderful, warm, strong, furry way of his.

Meanwhile we climbed and wheezed our way (Dany later said she thought her lungs were on fire) up through scrubby, spiky bush (as in Australian outback but colder and without the lethal snakes or spiders) of evergreen oak and juniper bushes into a majestic forest of sweet chestnuts. Still we couldn't see the top but at least we knew we were on the right track because from time to time there were those nice little red-and-white markers.

After precisely one hour of toiling upwards we found an excellent lunch stop in a clearing on the edge of the hill where the trees were thin enough to give incredible views of more and more trees and even higher and steeper mountain ranges. Lunch was a convivial and varied affair: Dany had salad with hard-boiled egg and onion slices lightly dressed with olive oil. Michèle had a flask of low-cholesterol broth. Véro had a baguette stuffed with ham and salad and all manner of good things and I had tuna and salad on organic rye bread followed by sesame seed paste on organic fig bread. We shared and compared, and discussed the relative merits of French as opposed to Swiss or Belgian chocolate and other weighty matters. 'I shall not look at the map,' I said lightly and jokingly. 'Ho, ho, it might spoil our lunch.'

Our bags were much lighter when we heaved ourselves to our feet again. 'Wait, I'll just look at the map now,' I said, and then asked 'Have we been past a ruined farmhouse?' No one had seen it. This meant that we had covered about one tenth of the day's journey and there was still as much uphill to go as we had already climbed. Despair gripped us. We reeled about on the path, hanging on to the trees in order not to topple down the slope we had so laboriously climbed up, gasping 'Oh no, it will be dark by the time we get there,' and 'How will we manage to get back?' (Dany again uncharacteristically giving in to panic, and completely forgetting we had two cars to get back in if ever we managed to get there.) Tension mounted when Michèle said 'Well, of course I knew we hadn't got very far, 2km at most,' and 'We didn't walk very fast, we'll have to do better than that for the rest of the day.' A sullen silence settled and we set off grinding our teeth – to find that around the next bend was the road which marked the halfway point of the whole trip (well, nearly half way – 4.5km out of 11.5km).

This was met with cries of joy and a massive improvement in our spirits. After a short debate whether to go right or left along the road (so much for my map reading) we went left, which was right, past a tourist information point which was probably also a splendid view point without even thinking about stopping ('Hilary would be ashamed of us'). And then I looked at the map again: 'Just after this we turn off to the right along the Trail – and go up for a little bit longer – and then it's DOWNHILL ALL THE WAY,' I said joyfully. I was nearly right. Being completely incapable of interpreting the contour lines on maps, I hadn't realised that the Trail did not actually go up any more at all, but plunged down off the road into a virtual abyss – so it was really and truly downhill all the way from there on.

The first bit was very steep and uncomfortable for those with short legs, particularly short legs that had just climbed 4.5km of steep uphill gradient. The path consisted of huge steps of ribbed slate, suitable for giants. My thighs began to tremble from the effort. (It was five days before I could walk up and down stairs normally again.) I was very glad we didn't have Kenneth with us after all. He wouldn't have been at his best here. He would have wanted to race and push us out of the way and knock us over and eat bushes. However, we could take our time and the further we went the nicer it got. The path very quickly evened out and was pleasant to walk on, there were beautiful views of distant mountain ranges at every corner, the sun was warm on our faces, and best of all it actually was downhill. We all became extremely mellow and content, and chatted leisurely about this and that and had a lovely time.

We came to a sweet little house nestling into the side of the hill with a swimming pool cut out of the hillside. Véro and I decided we wanted to live there. Leading up to the house was a real road. Real people were collecting pinecones by the side of the road. Further down the road there were real cars on the road and by the side of the River Gardon right down the bottom of the valley there were the traces of the dramatic floods of the previous September, with improbably huge trees lying uprooted alongside the tiny river.

And so we came to St Jean du Gard. It had taken us four hours altogether to walk from St Étienne Vallée Française, including our stop for lunch. We had excellent hot chocolate at the bar opposite the station. I mention this as it is very difficult to find decent hot chocolate in France and this is one of the rare places where it is a) hot, b) chocolatey and c) served in nice round cups which are just right for warming your hands around.

Although this last journey was just a few hours (excluding the hot chocolate), it felt in a way more significant than that: it was the end of the road, the end of an era almost, as doing the Stevenson Trail had become an important part of my life, and now it was over. The sense of achievement was succeeded by a feeling of loss – followed by a new wave of enthusiasm. I rang Hilary on reaching home: 'How about the Camino de Santiago de Compostela?' Not only is it just as lovely, it is ten times longer so it could be an ongoing project not for a mere four years but for the next forty. That should keep us busy.

Bridge over the River Gardon at St Jean du Gard.

TAILPIECE

Farewell Modestine

For twelve days we had been fast companions; we had travelled upwards of a hundred and twenty miles, crossed several respectable ridges, and jogged along with our six legs by many a rocky and many a boggy by-road. After the first day, although sometimes I was hurt and distant in manner, I still kept my patience; and as for her, poor soul! she had come to regard me as a god. She loved to eat out of my hand. She was patient, elegant in form, the colour of an ideal mouse, and inimitably small. Her faults were those of her race and sex; her virtues were her own. Farewell, and if for ever –

Robert Louis Stevenson
Travels with a Donkey in the Cévennes, 1878

Farewell Noisette, Jeep and Kenneth

For seventeen days (or four years) we had been intermittent companions; we had travelled upwards of 270km (including getting lost and repeating ourselves), crossed several respectable ridges and a couple of horrible ones, and jogged along with our twenty-six legs by many a rocky and many a boggy by-road. After the first day, although sometimes we were deeply fed up and distant in manner, we still kept our patience (mostly). And as for Noisette, Jeep and Kenneth – sensible souls! – they had come to regard us as nothing more than necessary appendages. They loved to eat, especially when it was inconvenient to us humans. They were resigned, sturdy, a delightfully furry brown when it wasn't raining, which it often was, and just the right height to prop ourselves up against when it all became too much. Their faults were, respectively, slowness, dislike of dogs, and speed; their virtues were tolerance (or was that boredom?) and readiness to carry our worldly goods. Farewell, but not for ever: the Camino de Santiago de Compostela is just around the corner –

Hilary Macaskill and Molly Wood, 2006

Dany in front of the church at Chasseradès.

FRENCH WORDS AND PHRASES

accueil chaleureux warm welcome

âne donkey

âne de Provence a breed of donkey originating in the Provence area of France

appellation d'origine contrôlée quality label usually confined to wine

Association 'Sur le Chemin de Robert Louis Stevenson' Friends of the Stevenson Trail

auberge inn

bât part of the donkey's harness: the wooden frame the panniers hang from

beignets fritters

beignets d'acacia acacia flower fritters

bête beast

Bête de Gévaudan mythical 'Beast of Gévaudan' which was widely considered to be responsible for the murder of several young women in the Gévaudan area of France in the 1800s

'Bien sûr. Je vois. Merci.' 'Of course. I see. Thank you.'

blanquette de veau veal stew in white sauce

boeuf bourguinon rich beef stew

bonjours hellos

boulangerie baker's

bourrée a lively dance

Brasserie du Musée Gilles' bar in Pradelles. Called a brasserie as he serves food as well.

Brevet Professionel Agricole professional agricultural diploma

brioche sweet yeasty bread or bun

'C'est compliqué.' 'That is difficult/ bothersome/annoying.'

calme calm

camaraderie jolly feeling of being great friends with everyone

'Certainement, c'était Noisette.' 'It certainly was Noisette.'

Cévennes mountainous area of Central France

Cévennols people from the Cévennes

Chemin de Stevenson Stevenson Trail

chou farci stuffed cabbage

clafoutis cross between a pancake and a tart and a cake

comestible eatable

confit de porc rich pork dish

crème anglaise thin egg custard

crêperie cafe specialising in pancakes

déchargement unloading

demain tomorrow

demi-pichet half a jug

'Deux. Et un chien. Et un âne.' 'Two people. And a dog. And a donkey.'

En Cévennes avec un âne n the Cévennes with a donkey

épicerie grocery

filet mignon small pork roast

fromage blanc cream cheese

garrigue open scrubland with stunted trees and limey soil

gastronomie grandiose excellent cooking

gentille nice-natured

gîte d'accueil bed-and-breakfast of a particularly welcoming sort

gîte (d'étape) bed-and-breakfast

Grande Randonnée (GR) official public footpath

grattons special sort of paté made with bits of pork squashed together

'Ici partit le 22 Septembre 1878 Robert Louis Stevenson pour son voyage à travers les Cévennes avec l'âne.' 'This is the starting point where Robert Louis Stevenson set out on his journey across the Cévennes with a donkey on 22 September 1878.'

Journal de Route en Cévennes the diary that Stevenson kept when he was actually walking the Trail

l'arbre à pain sweet chestnut tree

le Col du Pendu Hangman's Hill

lentilles vertes du Puy green lentils from Le Puy

'Les mettre dans la boîte là-bas.' 'Put it in the box over there.'

maison de retraite visitors' quarters

maligne cunning

maquis open scrubland with stunted trees and acid soil

menhir Stevenson large rock marking the Stevenson Trail

'Mon Dieu.' 'My God.'

montjoies de granite big granite stones

Musée du Cheval Horse Museum

nécessaire necessary

obligatoire mandatory

patron owner (when it's a man)

patronne owner (when it's a woman)

La Poste French equivalent of Royal Mail

producteur local local farmer

propriété privée private property

purée mush

raclette cheese-based dish from the Alps

'Rassurez vous, nous serons de retour ce soir.' 'Do not worry, we'll be back this evening.'

sage well-behaved

sans ânes without donkeys

sauce poulette chicken sauce

saucisses de Toulouse Toulouse sausages, big, fat meaty sausages on sale in all French butchers

saucisson garlic sausage

sentier découvert short footpath which is designed to be of particular interest concerning a specific item, usually carefully labelled e.g. footpath for looking at typical plants of the garrigue, each of which will have its name displayed

une modification a change

vente à la ferme farm produce for sale

vingt-cinq euros 25 euros

'Vous voulez nous accompagner?' 'Do you fancy coming along?'

HOW TO DO IT

How to get there
Rail Europe, 175 Piccadilly, London W1. Tel: 08708 371 371
www.raileurope.co.uk

Donkey-hire
Gilles Romand, Écuries du Musée, Place des Pénitents, 43420
  Pradelles. Tel: 04 71 00 88 88; email: gillesromand@wanadoo.fr
Other donkey-hirers (and places to stay with a donkey) are
  listed in the leaflet *Suivre les traces de R.L. Stevenson*,
  available from L'Association 'Sur le Chemin de Robert Louis
  Stevenson', 48220 Le Pont de Montvert. Tel/fax: 04 66 45 86 31;
  email: asso.stevenson@libertysurf.fr

Places we stayed
Goudet. Hôtel de la Loire. Tel: 00 44 71 57 16 83
Le Bouchet St Nicolas. L'Arrestadou. Tel: 00 44 71 57 35 34;
  fax: 00 44 71 57 30 93
Pradelles. Gîte d'étape. Tel: 04 71 00 88 88;
  email: gillesromand@wanadoo.fr
Cheylard l'Évêque. Le Refuge du Moure. Tel/fax: 00 44 66 69 03 21;
  email: gitap.simonet@wanadoo.fr
La Bastide Puylaurent. Gîte d'étape Nature Loisirs.
  Tel: 00 44 66 46 06 60
Notre Dame des Neiges. Hotellerie du Monastère. Only by
  reservation. Tel: 00 44 66 46 00 02
Chasseradès. Hôtel des Sources. Tel: 00 44 66 46 01 14;
  fax: 00 44 66 46 07 80; www.hotel-des-sources.fr
Le Bleymard. La Remise. Tel: 00 44 66 48 65 80; fax: 04 66 48 63 70
Le Pont de Montvert. Hôtel des Cévennes. Tel: 04 66 45 80 01
Barre des Cévennes. Gîte de la Croisete. Tel: 00 44 66 45 05 28
St Germain de Calberte. Le Petit Calbertois. Tel: 04 66 45 93 58;
  fax: 04 66 45 91 36; email:calbertois@bigfoot.com

Books

Travels with a Donkey in the Cévennes, Robert Louis Stevenson
(Oxford University Press, 1992)
Voyages avec un âne dans les Cévennes, Robert Louis Stevenson.
Photography Nils Warolin (Editions du Rouergue, Rodez, 1998)
Journal de Route en Cévennes (Éditions Privat Club Cévenol,
Toulouse, 1991)
Le Chemin de Stevenson (Fédération Française de la Randonnée
Pédestre, Comité Départemental de la Randonnée Pédestre
14, Bd Bourillon, 48002 Mende, France)
La Flore des Cévennes, Clément Martin, (Editions Espace Sud,
Montpellier, 1992)

Websites

www.chemin-stevenson.org. The official site of the Association
'Sur le Chemin de Robert Louis Stevenson'
www. ane-et-rando.com. Site of the Fédération Nationale Ânes et
Randonnée, with useful advice.

And if all this seems like too much effort, but you do like donkeys,
then visit The Donkey Sanctuary, Sidmouth, Devon EX10 0NU.
Tel: 01395 578222; www.thedonkeysanctuary.org.uk.

Countryside between Chasseradès and Le Bleymard.